DK
ANNUAL
2000

London • New York • Sydney • Delhi

DK

www.dk.com

Published in Great Britain by
Dorling Kindersley Limited,
9 Henrietta Street, London WC2E 8PS

2 4 6 8 10 9 7 5 3 1

Copyright © 1999 Dorling Kindersley Limited, London

All rights reserved. No part of this publication may be
reproduced, stored in a retrieval system, or transmitted
in any form or by any means, electronic, mechanical,
photocopying, recording or otherwise, without the
prior written permission of the copyright owner.

A CIP catalogue record for this book
is available from the British Library.

ISBN 0-7513-5824-X

Colour reproduction by Colourscan, Singapore
Dot Gradations, UK
Bright Arts, Hong Kong
GRB Editrice, Italy
Classic Scan, Singapore

Printed and bound by L.E.G.O. in Italy

Contents

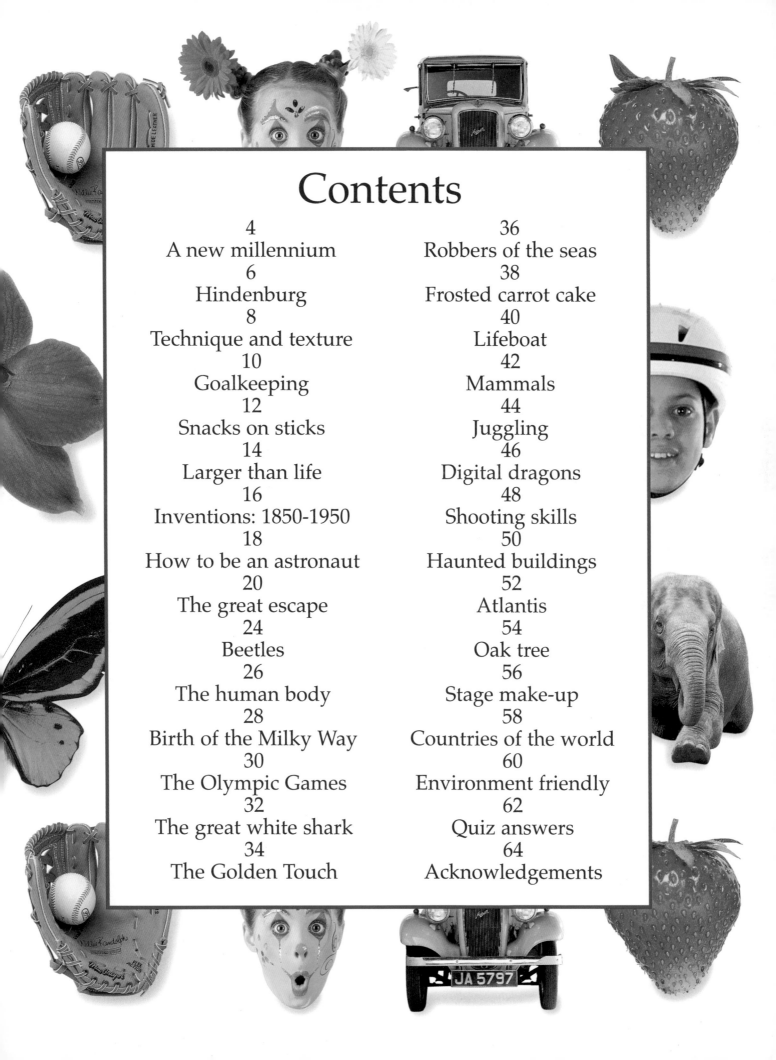

2000 FIRST DAWN OF THE NEW
MILLENNIUM IS IN THE ANTARCTIC

2000 A 24-HOUR PARTY IS
HELD IN NEW YORK, USA

2000 THE UK BUILDS A
GIANT CELEBRATORY DOME

A NEW MILLENNIUM

AS THE TWENTIETH CENTURY draws to a close, millennium fever has swept the globe. In some countries, such as the Arab states, Israel, and Japan, where other calendars are used, it is, of course, something of a non-event. Iran has even banned millennium celebrations altogether. But, for much of the world, plans are on course and a bewildering array of millennium projects are being hatched. However, with an estimated population of 6.5 billion people and a growing environmental awareness, scientists are already beginning to grapple with potential problems in the 21st century.

THE SITE OF CERN

Fuel of the future

Scientific fact and fiction merged at the end of 1995 when the first complete atoms of anti-matter were created at Switzerland's European Laboratory for Particle Physics (known as CERN). Anti-matter releases enormous bursts of energy, making it a potential fuel source.

Hotel is shaped like a sail

It's a wind-up!

This clockwork radio, designed by British inventor Trevor Baylis, offers a simple solution to an old problem. It does not need batteries or electricity and is therefore ideal for use in remote areas with no electricity supply in developing countries.

Aerodynamic hotel

The world's tallest hotel is taking shape in the Arab sheikdom of Dubai. It is the centrepiece of a huge new beach resort complex which will incorporate marina, waterpark, and sports and conference centres. The 321-m (1,053-ft) high hotel has 56 storeys and three basements below sea level. Designed in an aerodynamic sail shape, it is located on its own artificial island, which is linked to the mainland by a road bridge.

MODEL OF
DUBAI HOTEL

Under construction

After more than 100 years, the gigantic, Neo-Gothic Sagrada Familia church in Barcelona, Spain, is still a building-site. Although construction began in 1882, it remains a shell. The designer, the famous Catalan architect Antonio Gaudí, who died in 1926, predicted it would take two centuries to complete. Even uncompleted, the church is a magnificent architectural achievement.

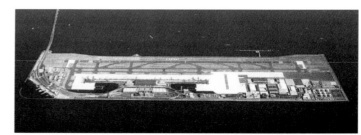

Airport on an island

A special artificial island 4.5 km (2.8 miles) long and 2.5 km (1.5 miles) wide was built in Osaka Bay to house Japan's new Kansai International Airport. It is connected to the overcrowded mainland by a six-lane highway and a railway. The vast steel and glass terminal was designed to withstand both earthquakes and typhoons.

2000 CATHOLICS CELEBRATE THE
MILLENNIUM IN THE VATICAN CITY

2000 ARTISTS DECORATE THE
AVENUES IN PARIS, FRANCE

2000 AUSTRALIA STAGES
THE SUMMER OLYMPICS

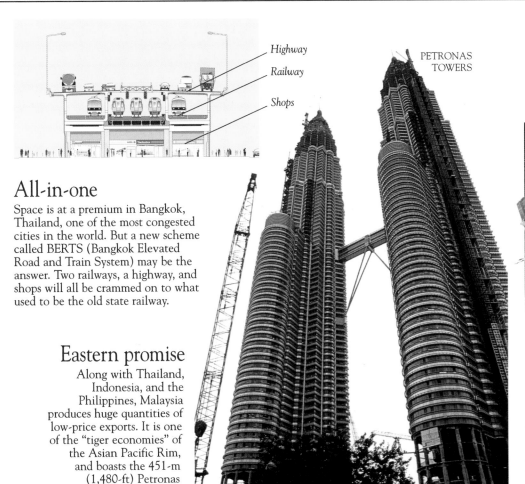

Highway

Railway

Shops

PETRONAS
TOWERS

AN ARTIST'S
IMPRESSION
OF *ALPHA*

All-in-one

Space is at a premium in Bangkok, Thailand, one of the most congested cities in the world. But a new scheme called BERTS (Bangkok Elevated Road and Train System) may be the answer. Two railways, a highway, and shops will all be crammed on to what used to be the old state railway.

Eastern promise

Along with Thailand, Indonesia, and the Philippines, Malaysia produces huge quantities of low-price exports. It is one of the "tiger economies" of the Asian Pacific Rim, and boasts the 451-m (1,480-ft) Petronas Towers, the world's tallest buildings.

New space age

Work is starting on a new International Space Station (ISS), code-named *Alpha*, which will provide a permanent orbiting research complex in the unique, nearly zero-gravity environment of space. In a new spirit of international co-operation, the project is jointly financed and organized by Russia, Japan, Europe, and the United States. The station will take 44 assembly flights to build and is due for completion in 2004.

CONCEPT 2096

Car date 2096

Concept 2096, designed to celebrate 100 years of the British motor industry, shows what cars might look like in the new millennium. It is computer-controlled and will reach speeds of 483 km/h (302 mph), with no driver, no steering wheel, and no brakes. It can also change shape and colour.

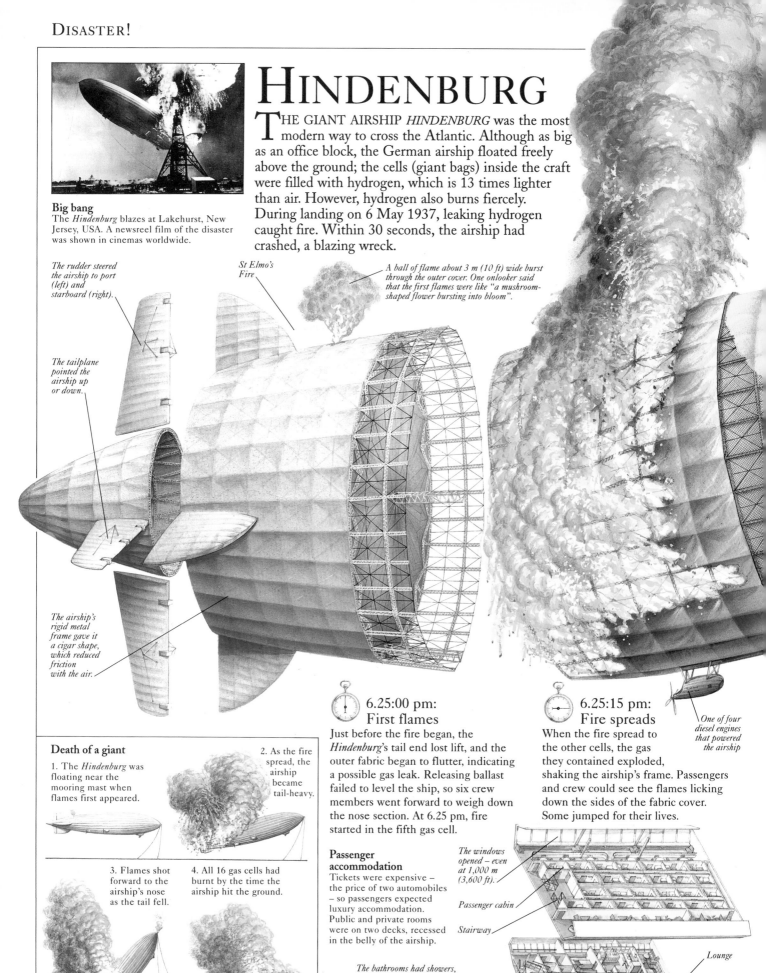

Big bang
The *Hindenburg* blazes at Lakehurst, New Jersey, USA. A newsreel film of the disaster was shown in cinemas worldwide.

HINDENBURG

THE GIANT AIRSHIP *HINDENBURG* was the most modern way to cross the Atlantic. Although as big as an office block, the German airship floated freely above the ground; the cells (giant bags) inside the craft were filled with hydrogen, which is 13 times lighter than air. However, hydrogen also burns fiercely. During landing on 6 May 1937, leaking hydrogen caught fire. Within 30 seconds, the airship had crashed, a blazing wreck.

The rudder steered the airship to port (left) and starboard (right).

St Elmo's Fire

A ball of flame about 3 m (10 ft) wide burst through the outer cover. One onlooker said that the first flames were like "a mushroom-shaped flower bursting into bloom".

The tailplane pointed the airship up or down.

The airship's rigid metal frame gave it a cigar shape, which reduced friction with the air.

Death of a giant

1. The *Hindenburg* was floating near the mooring mast when flames first appeared.

2. As the fire spread, the airship became tail-heavy.

3. Flames shot forward to the airship's nose as the tail fell.

4. All 16 gas cells had burnt by the time the airship hit the ground.

6.25:00 pm: First flames
Just before the fire began, the *Hindenburg*'s tail end lost lift, and the outer fabric began to flutter, indicating a possible gas leak. Releasing ballast failed to level the ship, so six crew members went forward to weigh down the nose section. At 6.25 pm, fire started in the fifth gas cell.

Passenger accommodation
Tickets were expensive – the price of two automobiles – so passengers expected luxury accommodation. Public and private rooms were on two decks, recessed in the belly of the airship.

6.25:15 pm: Fire spreads
When the fire spread to the other cells, the gas they contained exploded, shaking the airship's frame. Passengers and crew could see the flames licking down the sides of the fabric cover. Some jumped for their lives.

One of four diesel engines that powered the airship

The windows opened – even at 1,000 m (3,600 ft).

Passenger cabin

Stairway

The bathrooms had showers, but the spray was feeble and a timer limited water use.

Lounge

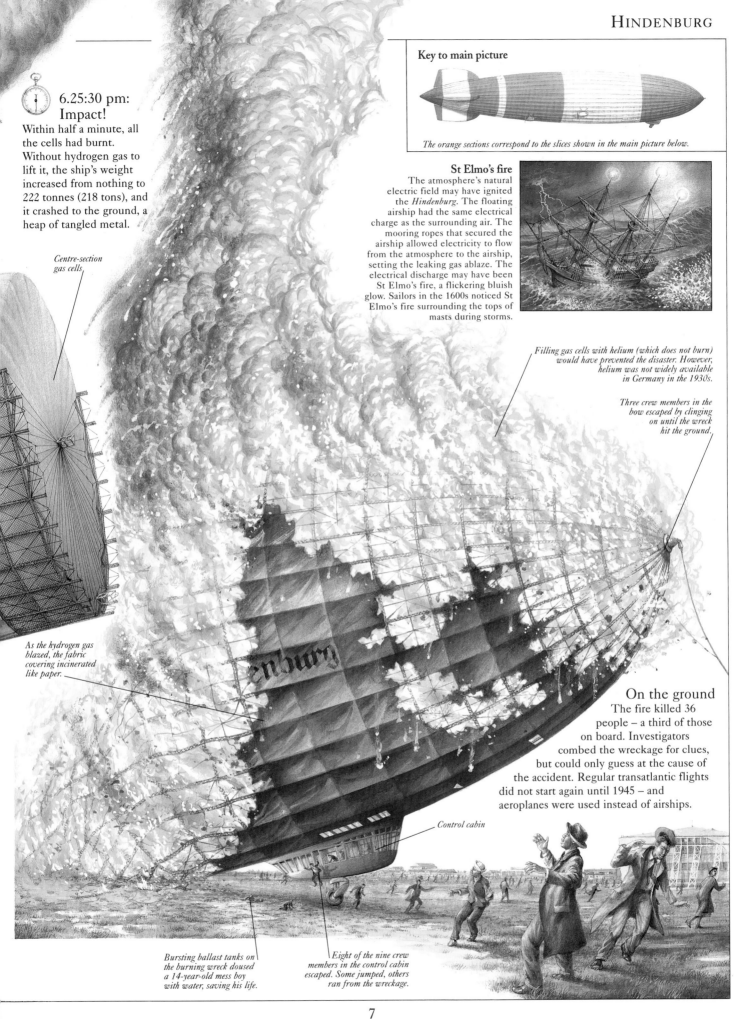

6.25:30 pm: Impact!
Within half a minute, all the cells had burnt. Without hydrogen gas to lift it, the ship's weight increased from nothing to 222 tonnes (218 tons), and it crashed to the ground, a heap of tangled metal.

Centre-section gas cells

Key to main picture

The orange sections correspond to the slices shown in the main picture below.

St Elmo's fire
The atmosphere's natural electric field may have ignited the *Hindenburg*. The floating airship had the same electrical charge as the surrounding air. The mooring ropes that secured the airship allowed electricity to flow from the atmosphere to the airship, setting the leaking gas ablaze. The electrical discharge may have been St Elmo's fire, a flickering bluish glow. Sailors in the 1600s noticed St Elmo's fire surrounding the tops of masts during storms.

Filling gas cells with helium (which does not burn) would have prevented the disaster. However, helium was not widely available in Germany in the 1930s.

Three crew members in the bow escaped by clinging on until the wreck hit the ground.

As the hydrogen gas blazed, the fabric covering incinerated like paper.

On the ground
The fire killed 36 people – a third of those on board. Investigators combed the wreckage for clues, but could only guess at the cause of the accident. Regular transatlantic flights did not start again until 1945 – and aeroplanes were used instead of airships.

Control cabin

Bursting ballast tanks on the burning wreck doused a 14-year-old mess boy with water, saving his life.

Eight of the nine crew members in the control cabin escaped. Some jumped, others ran from the wreckage.

Technique and texture

What tools and objects can you paint with, apart from a brush? Look for things around your home that could be used to create textures and patterns. Lay down lots of newspaper. Then move around a large piece of paper on the floor, and try using a variety of marks and gestures to make an abstract painting. Experiment with thick and thin paint. Can you invent new techniques and effects of your own?

Dabbing
Try a toothbrush for short dabs.

Blowing
A blob of thin paint can be blown across the paper with a drinking-straw.

Rolling
A decorating roller can be used to make long sweeping marks.

Thickening paint
Thick paint will add texture to your painting. Water-based paints can be thickened with PVA glue.

Dripping
Drip paint randomly across the paper from a yoghurt pot with a small hole in the bottom.

1 You can buy ready-mixed, water-based paints in large, squeezy bottles. These are good for painting a large picture. Find a bowl in which you can mix the glue and paint.

2 Put some ready-mixed paint into the bowl and then add the PVA glue in small amounts. Stir the glue in until you have just the thickness of paint you want.

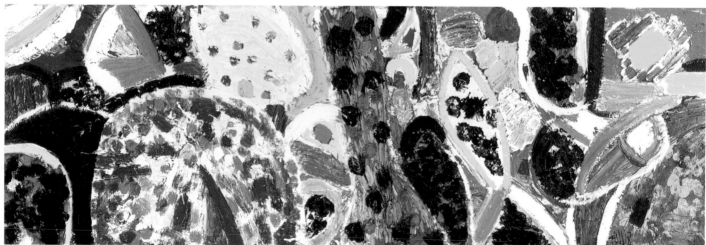

GILLIAN AYRES *Salix* 1991

The English artist Ayres uses very thick paint and brilliant colours for her highly textured paintings. The paint is so thick that it stands out from the canvas. *Salix* means "willow" – which gives us a clue to the theme of the painting. Can you see a fish and a waterlily leaf?

Marks and gestures
Thick strokes, short dabs, round blobs, and broad patches all go in different directions, creating a fascinating surface.

SHARON PETERS *Farewell* 1993

Combing
Use different objects to make patterns of thick and thin lines in the paint. A piece of card is good for spreading a big blob of paint smoothly on to the paper. Use an old comb, or another tool, to make marks in the paint.

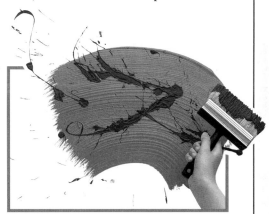

Brushing and flicking
Experiment with a big decorating brush. You need to have quite a lot of paint ready for this. Try flicking paint on to the paper with a smaller brush.

Action painting
Put some action into your painting by using fingers, hands, and feet to make marks. You can even run across your painting if you like.

Squirting and dribbling
Half-fill an empty washing-up liquid bottle with runny paint (with the help of a funnel). Dribble thin lines and marks, or try squeezing and squirting the paint.

Sponging
Use a sponge for making soft, smudgy effects and shapes. Experiment with using different amounts of paint on your sponge.

Goalkeeping

I F YOU ARE a goalkeeper you will need to develop quick reactions, excellent concentration, and good handling skills. Unless you save goals, you can never hope to be described as a good goalkeeper. You will perform skills unique to goalkeeping such as diving saves and punches to the ball, and use tactics which make it difficult for the attackers to score. As well as saving the ball you will also need to learn how to clear the ball from the goal area.

Hold the ball with one of your hands behind the ball and one of your hands on top.

Saving a low shot

When an attacker shoots a low ball you must dive to save it. As the ball approaches, dive sideways to form a barrier, then fall on top of it. Not only will your body form a wall, but your legs will also form an obstruction. Pull the ball tightly to your body to avoid the risk of a rebound into the path of an opponent.

Diving save

Here Gary Lineker has had a clear run at the goal and has shot from just inside the box. The goalkeeper has been forced to dive across the goal to reach the ball. His arms are stretched and ready to bring the ball close to his body.

Goalkeeper's punt

1 To bring the ball back into play use either a goal kick (a long-range kick from the goal area), a drop kick, or a punt. A punt involves kicking the ball after it has been dropped from your hands. This allows the ball to travel over a great distance. A drop kick involves the same basic principles, but you should not strike the ball until it has hit the ground. To perform a drop kick or a punt, hold the ball out in front of your body. Bend your knees, and look to check where your team-mates are on the pitch.

"For a goalkeeper, positioning is everything."
(Lev Yashin, Russian goalkeeper)

2 Drop the ball and watch it fall, keeping your head steady. Don't allow yourself to be distracted.

Total concentration on the ball is most important at this stage.

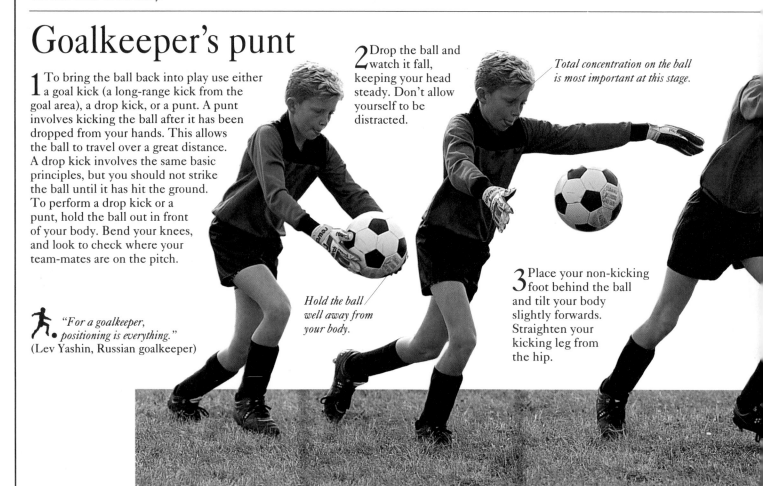

Hold the ball well away from your body.

3 Place your non-kicking foot behind the ball and tilt your body slightly forwards. Straighten your kicking leg from the hip.

Narrowing the angle

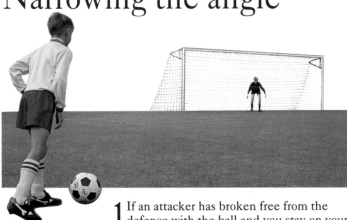

The goal looks very big to the attacker.

1 If an attacker has broken free from the defence with the ball and you stay on your goal line, you will give your opponent a large area at which to shoot.

2 Move steadily away from your goal line towards the ball. This will reduce the area of the goal at which your opponent has to shoot. Your timing and positioning must be exact. If you come out too soon, your opponent can dribble round you and score; if you come out too far, your opponent may chip the ball over your head.

Punching the ball

When you punch the ball away you must aim for height and distance to give your team-mates time to regroup. Clench your fists together and keep your wrists firm. As the ball comes towards you, punch the bottom half of the ball as hard and high as you can.

Saving the ball

Here Romanian goalkeeper Silviu Lung has punched the ball straight over Gary Lineker's head to stop him scoring. The match was a World Cup qualifier in 1985.

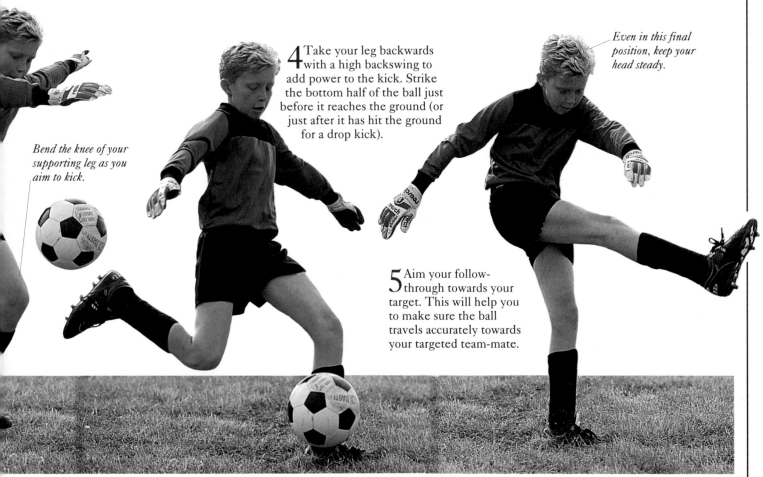

Bend the knee of your supporting leg as you aim to kick.

4 Take your leg backwards with a high backswing to add power to the kick. Strike the bottom half of the ball just before it reaches the ground (or just after it has hit the ground for a drop kick).

Even in this final position, keep your head steady.

5 Aim your follow-through towards your target. This will help you to make sure the ball travels accurately towards your targeted team-mate.

SNACKS ON STICKS

You can make simple kebabs with whatever you have at home. Try creating fruity ones, cheesy ones, or mixing sweet things with savoury things. Choose contrasting colours, and mix soft things with crunchy things. Here are some to try.

COOK'S TOOLS

Sharp knife • Potato peeler
Chopping board • Wooden skewers

You will need

(for 5 kebabs)

A carrot

Baby sweetcorn

Tinned mandarin oranges

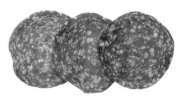

A green pepper

Small tomatoes

Strawberries

A small bunch of grapes

A hard cheese

Salami

Pineapple cubes

A peach

Mozzarella cheese

Stuffed olives

Baby mushrooms

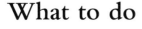

Small, cooked beetroots

Mangetout peas

Sliced ham

Cooked Frankfurter sausages

What to do

1 Cut the cheese and sausages into chunks. Cut cubes of green pepper. Cut the carrot in half and peel it into long strips.

2 Decide which things you want to go together and start threading them on to a wooden skewer, one at a time.

3 Carry on threading things on to the skewer until it is full, with just enough room at each end to hold it.

Rainbow kebabs

The finished kebabs are a good picnic or party treat. Slide everything off the skewer on to a plate with a fork. If not eaten at once, store in the fridge.

CHEESE AND PINEAPPLE

HAM AND FRUIT

FRUITY TREAT

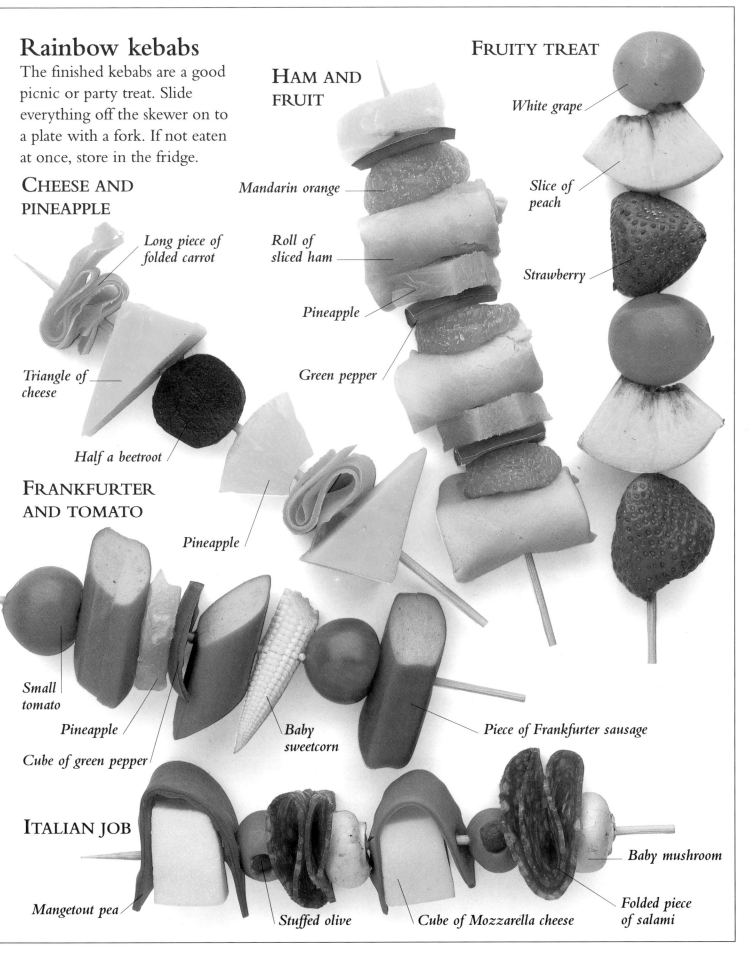

Long piece of folded carrot

Triangle of cheese

Half a beetroot

Mandarin orange

Roll of sliced ham

Pineapple

Green pepper

White grape

Slice of peach

Strawberry

FRANKFURTER AND TOMATO

Pineapple

Small tomato

Pineapple

Cube of green pepper

Baby sweetcorn

Piece of Frankfurter sausage

ITALIAN JOB

Baby mushroom

Mangetout pea

Stuffed olive

Cube of Mozzarella cheese

Folded piece of salami

LARGER THAN LIFE

If you were just 10 cm (4 ins) high, floorboards would stretch out like giant motorways, chairs would look like towering skyscrapers, and friendly family pets would turn into terrifying monsters. Hollywood has always been fascinated by the notion of small people, and has created imaginative films like *Honey, I Shrunk the Kids* where pocket-sized children trek across their garden, avoiding bumble bees, hosepipes, and the deadly lawn-mower along the way. To create such effects, various techniques are used, including outsize sets, giant props, and the use of blue screen.

SHRUNK TO FIT

One of the most innovative films to use outsize sets was the 1957 classic *The Incredible Shrinking Man*. Actor Grant Williams shrinks to micro-size after being caught in a radioactive mist. The ground-breaking visual effects used a mixture of outsize models and matte paintings to blend the actor into lifesize footage of kitchen floors and tables.

HANGIN' IN THERE

When miniature people have to appear to perform hair-raising stunts, the actors are often filmed in front of a blue screen projection which will later be replaced by background footage. One stunt for the film *The Borrowers* involved Jim Broadbent climbing down a kitchen shelf using a paper clip and some sewing thread. The sequence was shot on a studio sound stage using a giant tea cup prop.

VOYAGE OF DISCOVERY

In the 1966 film blockbuster *Fantastic Voyage*, Stephen Boyd and Raquel Welch travel through the bloodstream of a sick man, after being shrunk and injected into his arm. The film used state-of-the-art back projections to portray the vast interiors of the human body, and won Oscars for visual effects and set decoration.

Filmed background is added to actor's blue screen image

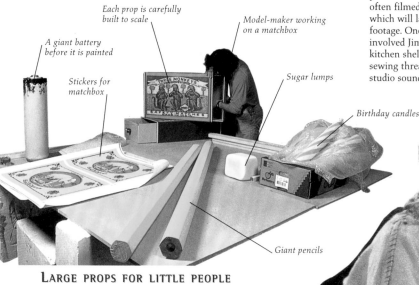

Each prop is carefully built to scale

Model-maker working on a matchbox

A giant battery before it is painted

Stickers for matchbox

Sugar lumps

Birthday candles

Giant pencils

LARGE PROPS FOR LITTLE PEOPLE

To create outsize props for the magical small world of the film *The Borrowers* (1997), the production designers had to build giant props to scale. Each ordinary object had to be constructed as it would have been seen or used by a little person only 10 cm (4 in) tall, so it was very important to use household items that would have interesting shapes when enlarged 14 times. The giant props (above) were created from polystyrene and foam and then painted.

TALL TALES

When the Jonathan Swift novel *Gulliver's Travels* was turned into a big budget television drama, the latest technology was used to bring to life both the tiny island of Lilliput and the giant world of Brobdingnag. Special sets were created to scale to make actor Ted Danson look minute in Brobdingnag, while blue-screen projections were used to show Danson towering above the miniscule Lilliputians.

IT'S A SMALL WORLD

Adapted from Mary Norton's famous children's books, *The Borrowers* tells the story of the Clock family, a group of tiny people who live under the floorboards of a big house and survive by "borrowing" things from the human family upstairs. The film contains a dazzling array of special effects which blend together the ordinary-sized world of the Borrowers and the huge outsize world of the house they inhabit. For the kitchen sequences, giant props were made by model-makers.

Faithfully re-created giant
pepper mill painted to look
like it is made from wood

China-effect sugar shaker
with Pod Clock's homemade
climbing gear hanging from it

Bendy drinking straws
were made from
lightweight plastic

A giant sticky sweet is among
the many "borrowed" items
collected by the Clocks

Inventions: 1850-1950

Q1. What did the Wright brothers do in 1903 that no-one had ever done before: fly an aeroplane, split the atom, or watch TV?

Long-playing record, 1948

Q2. Which was invented first, the telephone or the fax machine?

"Box telephone"

Q3. How long did the first LP (long-playing record) play on each side: 23 minutes, 33 minutes, or 53 minutes?

Hair dryer

Q4. In which year was the first hand-held hair dryer introduced in the United States: 1850, 1870, or 1920?

Q5. What does the car owe to the French Michelin brothers, André and Edouard?

Q6. Which invention, fitted to motor taxicabs in 1896, stopped passengers arguing with their drivers when they reached their destination?

Q7. Which was the first car to be built on a moving assembly line: the Model T Ford or the Benz Velo?

Q8. Was the first car built in Germany, the United States, or France?

Q9. Where did the world's first motorway, the Avus Autobahn, open in 1921: Germany, France, or the United States?

Q10. Electric toasters existed at the end of the 19th century, but when was the pop-up toaster invented: in about 1920, 1930, or 1940?

Q11. Emilé Berliner created the forerunner of modern records (discs). What did he invent so he could listen to them?

Q12. The first motorbike had a wooden frame and wooden wheels. Was it made in 1865, in 1885, or in 1905?

Q13. Which was invented first, the jet aeroplane or the helicopter?

First automatic photocopier

Q14. In which year did Chester Carlson invent the photocopier: 1859, 1903, or 1938?

An early motorcar

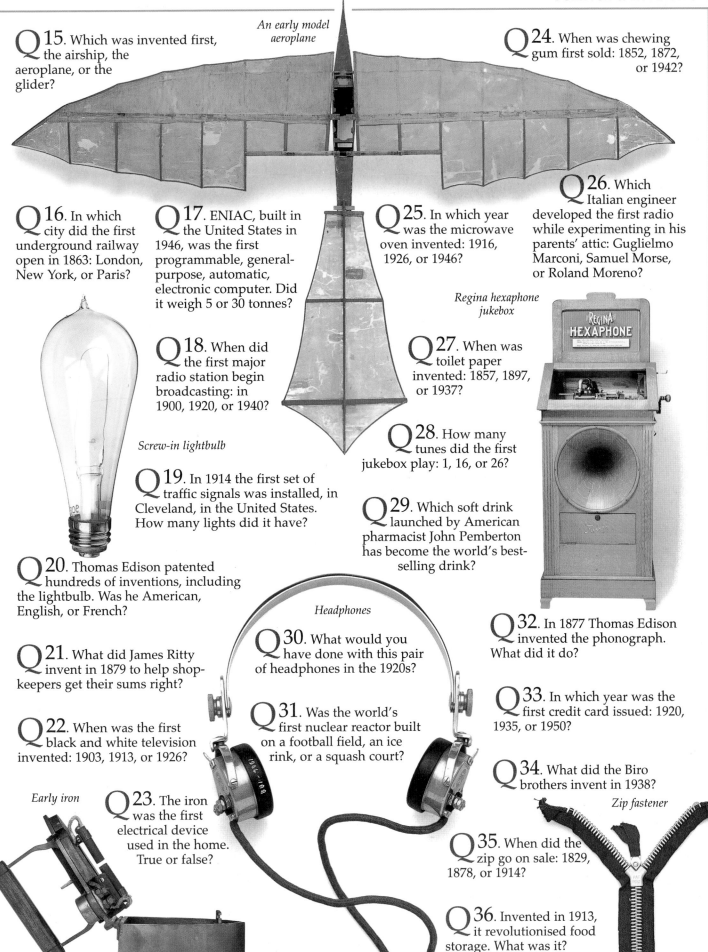

An early model aeroplane

Q15. Which was invented first, the airship, the aeroplane, or the glider?

Q24. When was chewing gum first sold: 1852, 1872, or 1942?

Q26. Which Italian engineer developed the first radio while experimenting in his parents' attic: Guglielmo Marconi, Samuel Morse, or Roland Moreno?

Q16. In which city did the first underground railway open in 1863: London, New York, or Paris?

Q17. ENIAC, built in the United States in 1946, was the first programmable, general-purpose, automatic, electronic computer. Did it weigh 5 or 30 tonnes?

Q25. In which year was the microwave oven invented: 1916, 1926, or 1946?

Regina hexaphone jukebox

Q18. When did the first major radio station begin broadcasting: in 1900, 1920, or 1940?

Q27. When was toilet paper invented: 1857, 1897, or 1937?

Screw-in lightbulb

Q19. In 1914 the first set of traffic signals was installed, in Cleveland, in the United States. How many lights did it have?

Q28. How many tunes did the first jukebox play: 1, 16, or 26?

Q29. Which soft drink launched by American pharmacist John Pemberton has become the world's best-selling drink?

Q20. Thomas Edison patented hundreds of inventions, including the lightbulb. Was he American, English, or French?

Headphones

Q32. In 1877 Thomas Edison invented the phonograph. What did it do?

Q30. What would you have done with this pair of headphones in the 1920s?

Q21. What did James Ritty invent in 1879 to help shop-keepers get their sums right?

Q33. In which year was the first credit card issued: 1920, 1935, or 1950?

Q31. Was the world's first nuclear reactor built on a football field, an ice rink, or a squash court?

Q22. When was the first black and white television invented: 1903, 1913, or 1926?

Q34. What did the Biro brothers invent in 1938?

Zip fastener

Early iron

Q23. The iron was the first electrical device used in the home. True or false?

Q35. When did the zip go on sale: 1829, 1878, or 1914?

Q36. Invented in 1913, it revolutionised food storage. What was it?

How to be an astronaut

SUSPENDED
As well as learning about spacecraft systems and the theory of working in space, astronauts must practise tasks in space conditions. They can learn what it is like to be in weightless conditions by scuba training or by using equipment like this harness which helps an astronaut get used to floating free.

MEN AND WOMEN ARE CHOSEN from around the world to train for travelling in space. They are launched aboard either the American shuttle, where English is the main language, or the Russian Soyuz rocket, where Russian is spoken. The preparations of the two space crews are similar. They involve classroom and practical training, including work in mock-ups of the orbiter, Spacelab, and Mir and in simulators such as the harness, the "5DF" machine, the moon-walker, and the multi-axis wheel, examples of which are found at the Euro Space Center, Transinne, Belgium, and are shown on these two pages. Astronauts can be selected for training every two years. They have a year's basic training, followed by training related to an astronaut's role in space, such as a pilot or mission specialist, who performs extra vehicular activity (EVA). Only then do the successful astronauts get assigned to a flight.

Harness helps astronaut prepare for weightlessness

Three Apollo astronauts in training before their flights to the Moon

JUNGLE EMERGENCY
Astronauts are trained for any kind of situation or emergency. These astronauts are gathering leaves and branches to make a shelter after a pretend emergency landing in the middle of the Panama jungle. Even after landing on Earth, an astronaut's journey may not be over.

LIFE RAFT
Astronaut candidates receive training in parachute jumping and land and sea survival. American astronaut Leroy Chiao floats in his life raft in training for an emergency departure from the space shuttle.

MOON-WALKER
Walking in a bulky spacesuit is difficult, particularly on the Moon where gravity is one-sixth of Earth's. The Apollo astronauts found bunny hops the best way to get around the lunar surface. Future trips to the Moon or to Mars can be prepared for by walking in a moon-walker, a suspended chair.

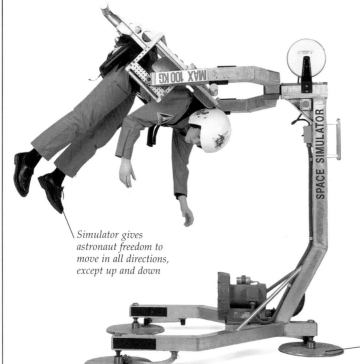

Simulator gives astronaut freedom to move in all directions, except up and down

FIVE DEGREES OF FREEDOM
Preparing for the weightlessness of space is not easy. The feeling can be simulated in a chair called the Five Degrees of Freedom (5DF) machine, which allows the astronaut to move in all directions, other than up and down, without restraint. Alternatively, astronauts can get a 20- to 30-second taste of weightlessness aboard a modified KC-135 jet aircraft as it dives from 10,668 m (35,000 ft) to 7,315 m (24,000 ft). But the experience is brief, even though it can be repeated up to 40 times a day.

Three "feet" float over the floor simulating movement achieved in frictionless space

UNDERWATER WEIGHTLESSNESS
Spacesuited astronauts can train for EVA in large water tanks, where the sensation of gravity is reduced. Space shuttle astronauts train with full-scale models of the orbiter payload bay and various payloads. Here some engineers work on a space station mock-up in preparation for future missions.

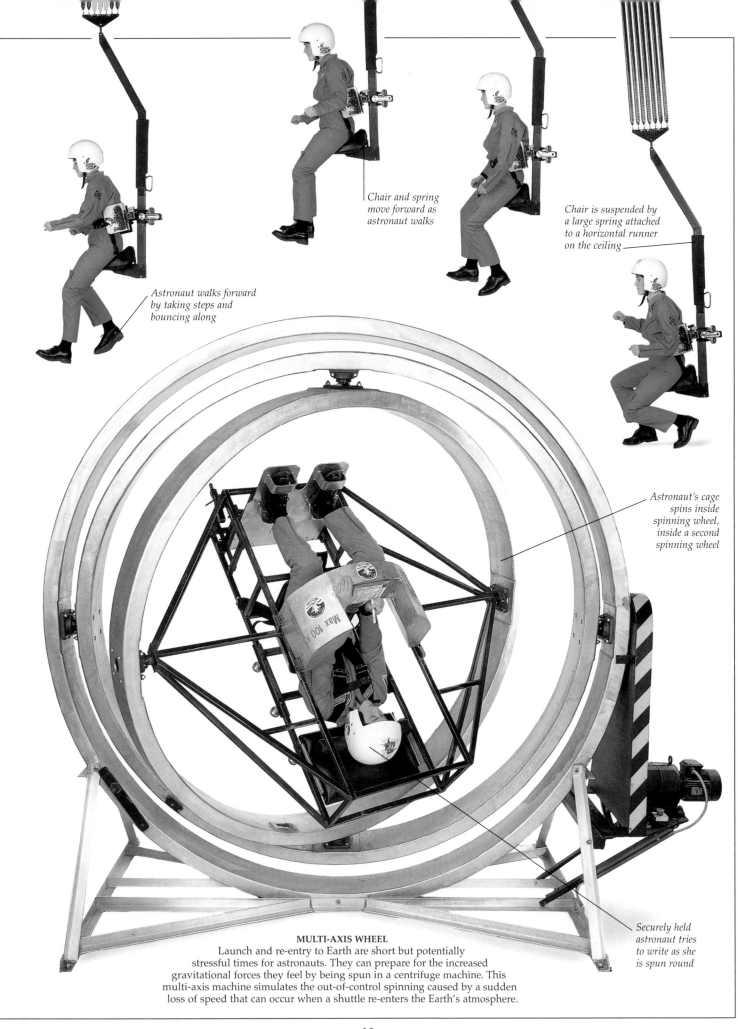

Chair and spring
move forward as
astronaut walks

Chair is suspended by
a large spring attached
to a horizontal runner
on the ceiling

Astronaut walks forward
by taking steps and
bouncing along

Astronaut's cage
spins inside
spinning wheel,
inside a second
spinning wheel

Securely held
astronaut tries
to write as she
is spun round

MULTI-AXIS WHEEL
Launch and re-entry to Earth are short but potentially
stressful times for astronauts. They can prepare for the increased
gravitational forces they feel by being spun in a centrifuge machine. This
multi-axis machine simulates the out-of-control spinning caused by a sudden
loss of speed that can occur when a shuttle re-enters the Earth's atmosphere.

THE GREAT ESCAPE

IN 1914, SIR ERNEST SHACKLETON SET out to cross Antarctica from coast to coast, a journey of 3,300 km (2,025 miles). Although his ship *Endurance* was wrecked before he set foot in Antarctica, he and his men pulled off the greatest

Midwinter celebration
Halfway through the Antarctic winter, on 22 June, Shackleton and his crew held a dinner on board *Endurance*. The room they nicknamed "the Ritz" was decorated with flags and bunting.

18 Jan 1915 STUCK FAST!
As howling gales drove the ice against the ship, the crew tried to free her using steam and sail.

The crew unloaded supplies down a canvas ramp.

CAMPING ON ICE
The months spent at Ocean Camp were hard. It was now summer, and the men's clothes and sleeping bags were always soaked through.

A LONG HARD HAUL
Lifeboats were hauled over the ice ridges and deep snow on sledges.

THE HUNTER HUNTED
There were many dangers on the ice. While out hunting seals and penguins, one of the men nearly became dinner for an enormous leopard seal.

27 Oct 1915 ABANDON SHIP!
Shackleton knew *Endurance* was doomed. The crushing ice had lifted the ship almost out of the water and forced her onto her side. He later wrote, "Huge blocks of ice, weighing many tons, were lifted into the air and tossed aside. We were helpless intruders in a strange world." Reluctantly, Shackleton gave the order to abandon ship.

escape in the history of polar exploration. Shackleton left South Georgia, an island in the South Atlantic Ocean, on 5 December 1914. At first *Endurance* made good progress, pushing her way through narrow channels ("leads") in the pack ice, and skirting round icebergs that towered above her decks. But on 18 January 1915 the wind shifted, closing the leads and packing the ice floes around the ship. She was stuck fast. During the long dark winter the pack ice carried the ship almost 1,000 km (600 miles) north. Finally her huge timbers snapped like matchsticks and icy water flooded into the holds, forcing the men to abandon ship. For the next six months the crew camped on drifting ice floes they named Ocean Camp and Patience Camp.

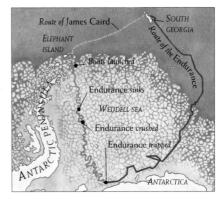

Shackleton's route south
The *Endurance* left the island of South Georgia in the South Atlantic Ocean in November 1914. She sank a year later, after being crushed by ice.

Seal blubber was used as fuel for the stove.

OUT TO DRY
The men dried their clothes on lines rigged across the ice.

WINTER NIGHTS
Huddled in their tents, the men played cards and read aloud.

The motion of the ice made some men seasick.

Tents were collapsed for packing.

TIME TO GO
When the men abandoned Patience Camp it was little more than a raft of rotting ice.

CRACK UP!
When Ocean Camp became unsafe, the men set up a new one on another ice floe. They called this camp "Patience Camp" because they had no choice but to wait for the ice to break up and free them. After three-and-a-half months the floe cracked and the crew hurriedly launched their boats.

ESCAPE FROM THE ICE
12 April 1916
As they left Patience Camp, the boats were spattered with bird droppings. It was the start of a difficult six-day journey across the Southern Ocean to Elephant Island.

> **EYEWITNESS**
>
> "In the event of my not surviving the boat journey to South Georgia you will do your best for the rescue of the party. You are in full command from the time the boat leaves this island."
>
> Ernest Shackleton's orders to Frank Wild before leaving Elephant Island
> 23 April 1916

18 April 1916 ELEPHANT ISLAND

After six days at sea the men scrambled ashore on a small rocky beach on Elephant Island. It was the first dry land they had stood on since they left South Georgia 16 months earlier. They were soaked to the skin and half-starved, but at least they were safe.

THE SNUGGERY

The men built a hut from two boats placed upside down on stone walls. They were packed inside like "sardines in a tin". On the island they had fresh water, and elephant seals and penguins to provide food and fuel.

STAYING IN TOUCH

On the stormy crossing to Elephant Island the crews of the three boats – *Stancomb Wills*, *Dudley Docker* and *James Caird* – fought hard to stay together. At any moment the boats could have been swamped by huge waves.

24 April 1916 FAREWELL

Six days after arriving at Elephant Island, Shackleton set sail in the 6-m (20-ft) *James Caird* with five companions. The nearest help lay at the whaling stations on South Georgia, 1,300 km (800 miles) away across the world's stormiest ocean. The men had to try and reach them. The ship's carpenter made a wood and canvas deck for the boat, which the men could crawl under to avoid the wind and spray. They took food for a month and two barrels of fresh water.

Sitting it out

The men left behind on Elephant Island suffered great hardship. When the seals and penguins left the island at the end of the summer, their stock of food and fuel soon ran low. Finally, they were forced to eat seaweed, limpets, and soup made of boiled seal bones. They had barely two days' food left when Shackleton, on board the ship *Yelcho*, arrived to rescue them.

ALL AT SEA

On the journey out through the pack ice the men slept in the boats. Occasionally a large ice floe provided a steady place for the cook to prepare a hot meal for the hungry men.

A ROUGH CROSSING

For 17 days the crew of the *James Caird* worked four-hour shifts, three at a time. Those off duty tried to rest in the cramped wet space below deck.

STORM AT SEA
When the wind eased, the men fought to break off the layers of ice that threatened to capsize the boat.

BAILING OUT
In one squall the boat was almost engulfed by the biggest wave they had ever seen, and the sea anchor broke away.

The sea anchor was made from three oars and a piece of canvas.

Vincent and McNeish were too weak to travel, so McCarthy was left with them while the other three set off across the mountains.

Shackleton used the axe to cut steps and ledges in the ice.

AN INCREDIBLE JOURNEY

Despite violent storms that almost sank their boat, the six men reached South Georgia in 17 days. But they had landed on the wrong side of the island. Between them and the whaling station at Stromness lay a range of mountains that had never been crossed. With just a makeshift axe and a short length of rope, Worsley, Shackleton, and Crean climbed over the mountains in 36 hours.

SLIDING HOME

20 May 1916
Holding on to one another like three tobogganers, the men slid down a snowfield to safety. A short time later, they staggered into the whaling station. They had made it.

All safe, all well
On 30 August 1916, after four failed rescue attempts, the Chilean naval ship *Yelcho* picked up Shackleton's men on Elephant Island. Not one life was lost on the expedition.

23

Beetles

THERE ARE AT LEAST 300,000 different kinds of beetle, living everywhere from snowy mountain tops to scorching deserts and muddy ponds. Beetles eat all kinds of plants and animals, dead or alive, and are eaten in vast numbers by birds, lizards, and small mammals. Although they may be pests, attacking crops and devouring stores of human food, beetles also play an important role in nature by eating dead plants and animals and returning them to the soil as valuable nutrients. All beetles undergo complete metamorphosis. Their eggs hatch into grubs, some of which feed and grow for several years before pupating and becoming adults. Adult beetles are the most heavily armoured of all insects. They have hardened front wings that meet in the middle to cover and protect the more delicate hind wings, which they use for flying. Beetles come in all sizes from tiny fungus beetles smaller than a pin-head, to the giant Goliath, up to 15 cm (6 in) long.

SACRED SCARAB
The ancient Egyptians believed that the scarab rolling her ball of dung symbolized the sun god Ra rolling the sun and renewing life.

GOLIATH
The African Goliath beetle (*Goliathus cacicus*) is the heaviest beetle in the world and one of the largest flying insects. The adults may be as long as 15 cm (6 in) and weigh up to 100 g (3.4 oz). The grubs live in rotting vegetation. After the adults emerge they fly up into the trees to feed on fruit and to mate.

Goliath beetle

Male Malayan frog beetle (*Sagra buqueti*)

Doryphorella langsdorfi

LEAF LIFE
Leaf beetles, like the two shown above, are often brightly coloured. The Malayan frog beetle (*Sagra buqueti*) uses its large hind legs to clasp a female during mating. The South American species (*Doryphorella langsdorfi*) lives and feeds on leaves.

Frog-like hind legs

Hairs deter predators

Jewel-like colours help conceal weevils on shiny green leaves

Lamprocyphus augustus

Brachycerus fascicularis

Pachyrhynchus species

STAG BEETLE
The powerful-looking jaws of this shiny black male stag beetle (*Mesotopus tarandus*) from Africa are probably used for fighting.

Stag beetle

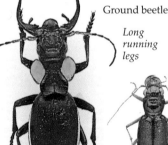

Ground beetle

Long running legs

Rostrum

Eupholus beccarii

Eupholus linnei

Tiger beetle

DARWIN'S BEETLE
It is said that this male stag beetle (*Chiasognathus granti*) bit the English naturalist Charles Darwin when he visited Brazil on the voyage of HMS Beagle. The beetle probably uses its long spiny jaws to threaten or fight other males.

Darwin's beetle

WEEVILS
Weevils are beetles that have a snout, or rostrum, with small biting jaws at the tip. Most weevils are plant feeders. Some may be brilliantly coloured and patterned, while others are hairy, possibly to deter predators. The middle three, from the Philippines, possibly mimic spiders.

KILLER BEETLES
Ground beetles and the closely related tiger beetles usually hunt and kill smaller insects for food. This large African species (*Anthia thoracica*) does not fly but scurries along the ground after its prey. The green tiger beetle (*Megacephala australis*) from Australia runs and flies in sunny places.

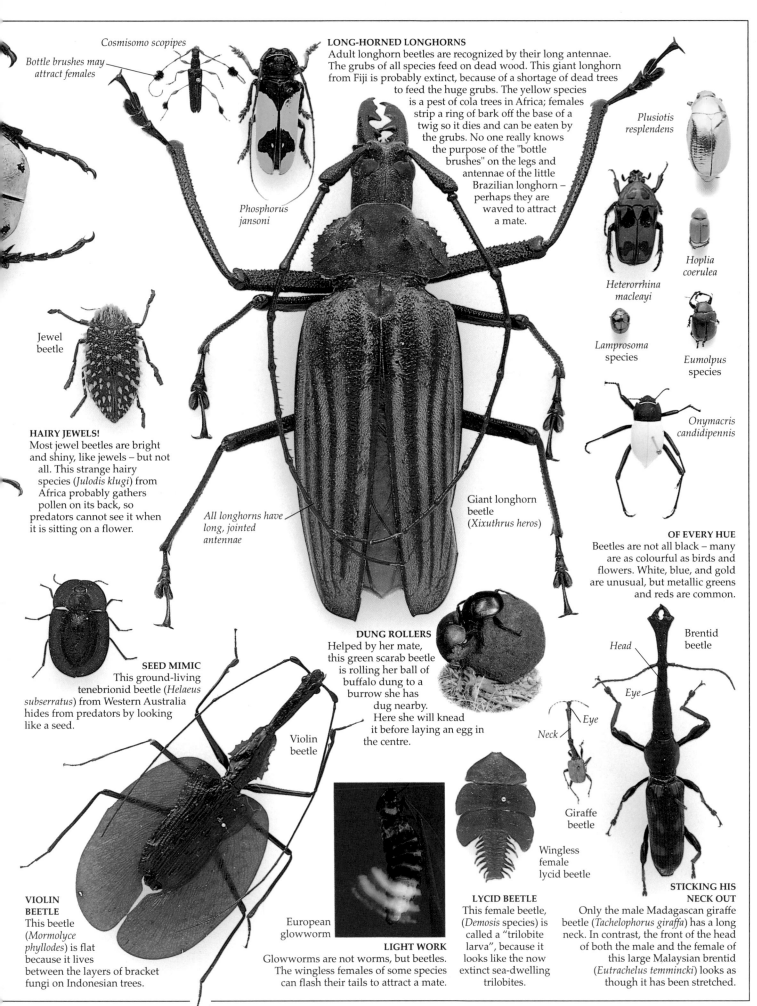

Bottle brushes may attract females

Cosmisomo scopipes

LONG-HORNED LONGHORNS
Adult longhorn beetles are recognized by their long antennae. The grubs of all species feed on dead wood. This giant longhorn from Fiji is probably extinct, because of a shortage of dead trees to feed the huge grubs. The yellow species is a pest of cola trees in Africa; females strip a ring of bark off the base of a twig so it dies and can be eaten by the grubs. No one really knows the purpose of the "bottle brushes" on the legs and antennae of the little Brazilian longhorn – perhaps they are waved to attract a mate.

Phosphorus jansoni

Plusiotis resplendens

Hoplia coerulea

Heterorrhina macleayi

Lamprosoma species

Eumolpus species

Jewel beetle

HAIRY JEWELS!
Most jewel beetles are bright and shiny, like jewels – but not all. This strange hairy species (*Julodis klugi*) from Africa probably gathers pollen on its back, so predators cannot see it when it is sitting on a flower.

Onymacris candidipennis

All longhorns have long, jointed antennae

Giant longhorn beetle (*Xixuthrus heros*)

OF EVERY HUE
Beetles are not all black – many are as colourful as birds and flowers. White, blue, and gold are unusual, but metallic greens and reds are common.

SEED MIMIC
This ground-living tenebrionid beetle (*Helaeus subserratus*) from Western Australia hides from predators by looking like a seed.

DUNG ROLLERS
Helped by her mate, this green scarab beetle is rolling her ball of buffalo dung to a burrow she has dug nearby. Here she will knead it before laying an egg in the centre.

Violin beetle

Head

Brentid beetle

Eye

Eye

Neck

Giraffe beetle

Wingless female lycid beetle

STICKING HIS NECK OUT
Only the male Madagascan giraffe beetle (*Tachelophorus giraffa*) has a long neck. In contrast, the front of the head of both the male and the female of this large Malaysian brentid (*Eutrachelus temmincki*) looks as though it has been stretched.

VIOLIN BEETLE
This beetle (*Mormolyce phyllodes*) is flat because it lives between the layers of bracket fungi on Indonesian trees.

European glowworm

LIGHT WORK
Glowworms are not worms, but beetles. The wingless females of some species can flash their tails to attract a mate.

LYCID BEETLE
This female beetle, (*Demosis* species) is called a "trilobite larva", because it looks like the now extinct sea-dwelling trilobites.

The Human Body

Q1. How many times does a heart beat every day: 100,000, 500,000, or 1,000,000 times?

Q2. Who has more bones: a child or an adult?

Q3. What is the hardest substance in the human body?

Components of the chest

Q4. How much air can the lungs hold: 3, 10, or 15 litres (5, 18, or 26 pt)?

Q5. Which country has more hospitals than any other?

Q6. Can you name the horny substance in nails, hair, and skin?

Q7. Can you name the female organ in which a baby develops?

Q8. Which is the largest organ of the human body?

Q9. Which doctor founded psychoanalysis, a treatment for mental illness?

Q10. Can you name the bony cage that protects the chest organs?

Q11. In how many directions can the knee joint bend?

Leg and foot bones

Q12. Which intestine is longer: the small intestine or the large intestine?

Q13. How many muscles are there in the human body: 200, 400, or over 600?

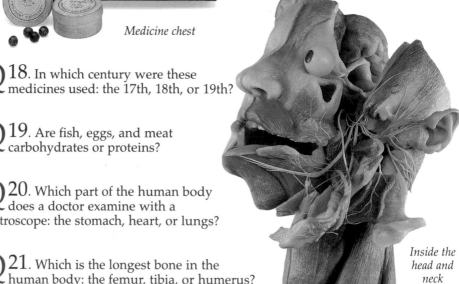

Tropical papayas

Q14. The tropical fruit papaya can be used to treat threadworms and ringworms. True or false?

Q15. In which year were X-rays discovered by Wilhelm Roentgen: 1800, 1850, or 1895?

Thoracic vertebra

Q16. In which part of the human body would you find this bone?

Q17. How heavy is the human head: 2 kg, 4 kg, or 8 kg (4.4 lb, 8.8 lb, or 17.6 lb)?

Medicine chest

Q18. In which century were these medicines used: the 17th, 18th, or 19th?

Q19. Are fish, eggs, and meat carbohydrates or proteins?

Q20. Which part of the human body does a doctor examine with a gastroscope: the stomach, heart, or lungs?

Q21. Which is the longest bone in the human body: the femur, tibia, or humerus?

Inside the head and neck

Q22. Which French scientist developed vaccines and invented pasteurisation (heating to destroy bacteria)?

Q23. How many bones are there in the human body: 106, 206, or 306?

Q24. Which Polish-born French woman discovered the chemical element radium and was awarded the Nobel Prize for chemistry in 1911?

Q25. What is the difference between a local anesthetic and a general anesthetic?

Q26. Who discovered penicillin?

Q27. What is the function of arteries?

Q28. Why did doctors apply bloodsucking leeches to their patients?

Leeches

Q29. When did Elizabeth Garrett Anderson become the first woman graduate from medical school in Britain: 1810, 1876, or 1934?

Q30. In England before 1600 why did human dissection take place in secret?

Q31. What did a doctor do with this saw at the Battle of Waterloo?

Q32. Can you name 2 of the major blood groups?

Saw and glove

Q33. How many muscles does the average adult use when going for a walk: 50, 100, or over 200?

Q34. Which ancient form of Chinese medicine involves the insertion of needles into various points of the body to treat illnesses?

Q35. In which year was the first test tube baby born: 1978, 1986, or 1990?

Q36. Where is the smallest bone in the human body: in the ear, the foot, or the wrist?

Q37. When was the first successful heart transplant performed: 1937, 1967, or 1987?

Q38. When did dentistry become a recognised profession: in the 15th, 17th, or 19th century?

Q39. Which fluid secreted by the liver aids digestion?

Q40. What does a midwife do?

Q41. Which instrument does a doctor use to listen to the heart and lungs?

Q42. In which year was the syringe first used to inject drugs directly into the body: 1753, 1853, or 1953?

Human skeleton

Hypodermic syringe

Q43. How many bones are there in the hand: 12, 20, or 27?

Q44. In which year was the World Health Organisation (WHO) set up by the United Nations: 1908, 1928, or 1948?

Q45. Can you name the bone to which the ribs are attached?

Q46. Can you name 2 of the 5 main senses of the human body?

Q47. Why do people get goose bumps?

Q48. When were anesthetics introduced: in the 1840s, 1880s, or 1920s?

Ether inhaler

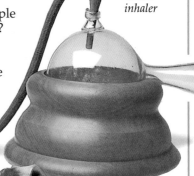

Birth of the Milky Way

Astronomers can date when the big bang took place, but can only guess that the galaxies formed about half a billion years later. Their instruments cannot record the subtle coming together of gas clouds that resulted in the creation of billions of galaxies. Fortunately, youthful galaxies undergo violent outbursts that can be witnessed halfway across the Universe – but after that, they settle down. And that's lucky for us, for we live in such a galaxy. This is the story of our Milky Way from its own birth to the day it created the Sun and planets.

Our Galaxy is born as countless warm gas clouds come together under the pull of gravity. Stars are born as clouds collide.

A great deal of gas starts to accumulate in the galaxy's core. Its gravity becomes so great that a massive black hole forms and grows.

Gas and stars spiral into the black hole, forming a superhot whirlpool called an accretion disc. This brilliant disc is a quasar.

Cross-section of the quasar's accretion disc and its high-speed jets

The jets from a radio galaxy billow out into huge clouds.

A violent youth

In its youth, the centre of our Galaxy probably flared into life as a quasar. A quasar is the tiny, dazzling core of a very young and active galaxy. At its heart is a supermassive black hole, voraciously gobbling gas – and shooting what it doesn't eat far out into space. Astronomers have found thousands of quasars, most so remote they look like very faint stars.

A quasar sends out two jets of charged particles at almost the speed of light.

The quasar has evolved into a radio galaxy

A CHANGING UNIVERSE

When astronomers look out to great distances, they are looking back in time, to the Universe as it was in its youth. They find that many more distant galaxies have quasars at their core than nearby galaxies. So the Universe is changing with time, as the Big Bang theory predicts. This rules out theories that suggest the Universe is infinitely old and unchanging.

Quasar

The early Universe (small sphere) contains many more quasars and radio galaxies than the Universe of today (large sphere).

MARTIN RYLE

In the late 1950s, the British astronomer Martin Ryle (1918-1984) used a radio telescope that he and his team had built at Cambridge to look at galaxies in the distant Universe. He came up with the first evidence that galaxies were more tightly packed together in the past, and that the young Universe was dominated by quasars.

GROWING LESS VIOLENT

Our Galaxy's quasar phase lasted for only a few million years. Next, it embarked on a less violent phase, as a radio galaxy. The jets it beamed out as a quasar billowed out into two enormous clouds, generating powerful radio waves. There was still potential for outbursts from the core – the black hole was there, lurking – but as gas was used up to make stars, the black hole was slowly starved.

The radio-emitting jets can span more than a million light years.

SETTLING DOWN

Nine billion years after its fiery birth, our Milky Way was starting to settle down. A huge black hole, weighing in at three million star masses, still lurked at its core; but it was quiescent, for gas fodder was not as plentiful as before. The Galaxy had by now given birth to billions of stars, arranged in a beautiful spiral shape 100,000 light years across. But there was always room for more.

Pillars of starbirth: young stars emerging from a pillar of dust and gas in the Eagle Nebula about 7,000 years ago.

A STAR IS BORN

Some 4.6 billion years ago, a cloud of dust and gas started to collapse in an anonymous suburb of the Milky Way. As it shrank, it spun faster, eventually becoming a disc. At its heart, it grew hotter and denser, until the core flashed into life. A star, our Sun, had been born. Powered by nuclear fusion reactions, the young Sun showered light and energy onto its emerging family: the nine planets forming in the surrounding disc.

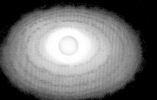

The young Sun forms in a disc of gas and dust.

The surrounding disc condenses into the planets, including Earth.

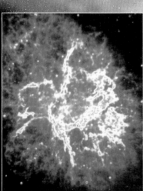

Crab Nebula: the remains of a dying star that blasted heavy elements across space.

STARTING WITH HYDROGEN . . .

All stars can combine the nuclei of hydrogen in their cores to make helium, a reaction that gives out energy. The heavier stars can also fuse three heliums to create carbon.

The heavy gang

George Gamow believed that all the elements were created in the Big Bang. But now we know that it made only the lightest – hydrogen, helium, and lithium. It turns out that the other 89 elements, making up just 1% of the total material in the Universe, were forged in the nuclear furnaces of stars. They were then scattered throughout space by stars shedding matter in their death throes.

. . . ENDING WITH IRON

Massive stars can create elements as heavy as iron in their cores. When they try to fuse iron, they explode as supernovas, blasting their outer layers into space. In the fury of the explosion, even heavier elements can be synthesized.

Three helium nuclei combine to form carbon.

Each helium nucleus consists of two protons and two neutrons.

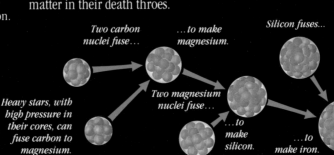

Two carbon nuclei fuse . . .

. . . to make magnesium.

Silicon fuses . . .

Heavy stars, with high pressure in their cores, can fuse carbon to magnesium.

Two magnesium nuclei fuse . . .

. . . to make silicon.

. . . to make iron.

The heaviest stars can fuse two nuclei of silicon to make iron.

THE OLYMPIC GAMES

OLYMPIC GAMES SUMMER VENUES

The modern Olympic Games, which began in 1896, were the brainchild of French scholar Pierre de Coubertin, who had been inspired by stories of the ancient Greek games. Every four years, athletes from all over the world meet to compete in the Summer Olympic Games. The only pauses since 1896 came in 1916, 1940, and 1944 when the games were cancelled as a result of war. Today, over 10,000 competitors take part in more than 20 sports.

YEAR	LOCATION
1896	Athens, Greece
1900	Paris, France
1904	St Louis, USA
1906	Athens, Greece
1908	London, UK
1912	Stockholm, Sweden
1920	Antwerp, Belgium
1924	Paris, France
1928	Amsterdam, Netherlands
1932	Los Angeles, USA
1936	Berlin, Germany
1948	London, UK
1952	Helsinki, Finland
1956	Melbourne, Australia*
1960	Rome, Italy
1964	Tokyo, Japan
1968	Mexico City, Mexico
1972	Munich, Germany
1976	Montreal, Canada
1980	Moscow, USSR
1984	Los Angeles, USA
1988	Seoul, South Korea
1992	Barcelona, Spain
1996	Atlanta, USA
2000	Sydney, Australia
2004	Athens, Greece

Equestrian events held in Stockholm, Sweden

LONGEST-STANDING CURRENT OLYMPIC TRACK AND FIELD RECORDS

EVENT	DISTANCE/ TIME/SCORE	COMPETITOR	COUNTRY	DATE
Men's long jump	8.90 m (29 ft 2.4 in)	Bob Beamon	USA	18 October 1968
Men's javelin	94.58 m (310 ft 4 in)	Miklos Nemeth	Hungary	25 July 1976
Women's shot	22.41 m (73 ft 6 in)	Ilona Slupianek	GDR	24 July 1980
Women's 800 m	1 min 53.43 sec	Nadezhda Olizarenko	USSR	27 July 1980
Women's 4 x 100 m	41.60 sec	Team event	GDR	1 August 1980
Men's 1500 m	3 min 32.53 sec	Sebastian Coe	GB	1 August 1980
Women's marathon	2 hr 24 min 52 sec	Joan Benoit	USA	5 August 1984
Men's 800 m	1 min 43 sec	Joaquim Cruz	Brazil	6 August 1984
Decathlon	8,847 points	Daley Thompson	GB	9 August 1984
Men's 5000 m	13 min 05.59 sec	Said Aouita	Morocco	11 August 1984

In the 1968 Olympics at Mexico, Bob Beamon added a staggering 55.25 cm (21.75 in) to the old long jump record, and won the competition by a lead of 72.39 cm (28.5 in). His jump of 8.90 m (29 ft 2.4 in) was the first beyond both 28 and 29 feet (8.53 and 8.84 m). The first 8.53 m (28 ft) jump in the Olympics was not until 1980, 12 years later.

FAMOUS OLYMPIC COMPETITORS

GENERAL PATTON George Patton (1885–1945), US World War II general, took part in the Modern Pentathlon at the 1912 Stockholm Games, coming fifth in the event. He might have won, but for the fact that shooting was his weakest sport!

DR SPOCK A member of the winning US rowing eights team at the 1924 Paris Olympics was Benjamin Spock (1903–1998), who later became famous as the author of *The Common Sense Book of Baby and Child Care* (1946), one of the bestselling books of all time.

TARZAN Johnny Weismuller (1904–1984), winner of swimming gold medals at the 1924 Paris Olympics and 1928 Amsterdam Olympics, went on to appear as Tarzan in numerous films.

LAST APPEARANCES OF OLYMPIC SPORTS

Each Olympic Games includes different, new sports. However, as new ones arrive, other sports are discontinued.

SPORT	LAST APPEARANCE
Cricket	Paris, 1900
Croquet	Paris, 1900
Golf	St Louis, 1904
Lacrosse	London, 1908
Motor boating	London, 1908
Tug-of-war	Antwerp, 1920
Rugby	Paris, 1924
Polo	Berlin, 1936

OLYMPIC DECATHLON EVENTS

The decathlon event, in which men only compete, has been included in every Olympic games since 1904. Ten different events make up the decathlon:

100 m • Long jump • Shot put • High jump • 400 m • 110 m hurdles • Discus • Pole vault • Javelin • 1500 m

AMAZING FACT! A number of decathletes have gone on to become film actors. Floyd Simmons, who was a bronze medallist in Helsinki in 1952, appeared in *South Pacific* (1958), and Bruce Jenner, a gold medallist in Montreal in 1976, found fame through his role in *Can't Stop the Music* (1980).

TOP INDIVIDUAL MEDAL WINNERS IN A SUMMER OLYMPICS CAREER

MEDALLIST	COUNTRY	SPORT	YEARS	GOLD	SILVER	BRONZE	TOTAL
Larissa Latynina	USSR	Gymnastics	1956–1964	9	5	4	18
Nikolay Andrianov	USSR	Gymnastics	1972–1980	7	5	3	15
Edoardo Mangiarotti	Italy	Fencing	1936–1960	6	5	2	13
Takashi Ono	Japan	Gymnastics	1952–1964	5	4	4	13
Boris Shakhlin	USSR	Gymnastics	1956–1964	7	4	2	13
Sawao Kato	Japan	Gymnastics	1968–1976	8	3	1	12
Paavo Nurmi	Finland	Athletics	1920–1928	9	3	0	12
Viktor Chukarin	USSR	Gymnastics	1952–1956	7	3	1	11
Vera Cáslavská	Czechoslovakia	Gymnastics	1964–1968	7	4	0	11
Carl Osborn	USA	Shooting	1912–1924	5	4	2	11
Mark Spitz	USA	Swimming	1968–1972	9	1	1	11

AMAZING FACT! The only event at which outstanding gymnast Larissa Latynina did not win a medal between 1956 and 1964 was the beam, in 1956. She came fourth!

DID YOU KNOW? The Olympic symbol is made up of five interlocking rings, standing for the continents of Europe, Asia, Africa, Australasia, and America.

MOST SUMMER OLYMPICS MEDALS

COUNTRY	GOLD	SILVER	BRONZE	TOTAL
USA	815.5	622	534	1,971.5
USSR	395	319	295	1,009.0
UK	165	215.5	213	593.5
France	161	172	187.5	520.5
Germany	147.5	173	178	498.5

AMAZING FACT! "Half medals" result when nationality is uncertain and they are shared between two countries.

MOST SUMMER OLYMPICS COMPETITORS

CITY	YEAR	COUNTRIES	COMPETITORS
Atlanta	1996	197	10,310
Barcelona	1992	172	9,364
Seoul	1988	159	9,101
Munich	1972	122	7,156
Los Angeles	1984	141	7,058
Montreal	1976	92	6,085
Mexico City	1968	112	5,530

ONE-OFF OLYMPIC EVENTS

As well as sports such as cricket, croquet, golf, lacrosse, polo, and rugby, which remain popular in many countries but are no longer included in the Olympics, there are a number of "oddity" sports that have appeared once or twice, but never again:

100 M SWIMMING FOR SAILORS Only members of the Greek navy could enter this event, included in the 1896 Athens Olympics.

JUMPING ON HORSEBACK Both long jump and high jump on horseback were included in the Paris Olympics in 1900.

UNDERWATER SWIMMING In this event, which appeared only once, in the 1900 Paris Olympics, contestants received extra points for the length of time they managed to stay submerged.

WATER OBSTACLE RACE In this unusual race, held at the Paris Games, 1900, swimmers had to swim under and climb over boats.

DUELLING Duelling pistol shooting was included in the Athens Games, 1906.

ARCHERY At Antwerp, 1920, archers used live birds as targets.

PARALYMPICS FACTS

WHAT ARE THE PARALYMPICS? The Paralympic Games are the Olympics for athletes with disabilities. They are held every four years, after the Olympic Games, and always at the same venue.

WHEN DID THEY START? The first Paralympics were held in Rome in 1960, with about 400 athletes from 23 countries. Until 1972, they were restricted to athletes with spinal injuries, but now include those with other disabilities. Winter Paralympics have been held since 1976.

NUMBER OF ATHLETES At the 1996 Atlanta Paralympics, 4,000 athletes from 118 countries competed.

CHAMPION GOLD MEDALLIST Louise Sauvage (Australia) won four gold medals at the 1996 Atlanta Games. She also won the Boston Wheelchair Marathon in both 1997 and 1998.

YOUNGEST COMPETITOR LeAnn Shannon (US) is the youngest person ever to compete in the Paralympic Games. Aged 13 at the time of the 1996 Atlanta Games, she won three gold medals and one silver, and holds the world record in the 400, 800, and 1,500 m wheelchair events.

The great white shark

A POWERFUL PREDATOR, the great white inspires fear. This awesome shark grows to over 6 m (20 ft) long and weighs more than 2 tonnes (2.2 tons). It is the largest of the predatory sharks, capable of eating seals whole. The great white became famous in the *Jaws* movies where it appeared as a blood-thirsty creature intent on killing people. Attacks on people are rare, and possibly occur when a shark mistakes a person for its usual seal prey. Despite its fame, little is known about the great white because it is rarely seen. Scientists have yet to discover where mating and birth occur, and their age when they reproduce or die. No-one knows how many great whites there are, but in some areas they may be on the decline.

FRENCH LANDING
This old engraving of a great white landed on France's Mediterranean coast shows how a century ago people were also fascinated by sharks. Unless they were lucky enough to see sharks first hand, artists had to rely on descriptions to make their drawings since there were no photographs. There are several inaccuracies in this engraving – the artist has given the great white the tail of a thresher and gill covers, like bony fish, as well as gill slits.

Dorsal fin

Small second dorsal fin, compared to size of first dorsal fin

Pelvic fin

Front view of model of a great white shark

Swimming keel

Long snout

Upper and lower lobes of caudal fin are almost symmetrical

Relatively small anal fin

Clasper

WARM BLOOD
Great whites and their relatives – the mako, thresher, and porbeagle – are all warm-blooded, which means that they are able to keep their body temperature higher than the surrounding water. Only mammals, birds, and a few fast fish, like the tuna, are warm-blooded. These sharks have blood vessels in their muscles arranged in complex nets, so that the warm blood leaving the muscles passes heat to the cool blood coming from the gills. A high body temperature means that great whites have warm muscles which are able to act fast. This is important for a predator that has to make a high-speed dash to catch its prey. Being warm-blooded may also help the great white to digest its food more quickly. Scientists estimate that after a big feed a great white can last three months before needing another meal.

Pore marking position of ampullae
of Lorenzini – sensory organs
for detecting prey's electric field

Long gill
slit – one
of five

Sharp,
serrated
teeth

WHITE DEATH
A great white's
colouring makes it
difficult to see in the
water, so it is able to
sneak up on its victims.
When seen from below, a
shark's white undersides
blend in with a bright sky's
reflection at the water's surface.
This magnificent shark is sometimes
called "white pointer", referring to its
pointed snout which makes it more streamlined. Great whites often have scratches and scars
on their snouts which may be the result of their prey
fighting back. They may also be bitten by larger members
of their own kind which move in to take bait away from them.

Full-length side view
of model of a male
great white shark

Pectoral fin

TAKING THE BAIT
Scientists, film-makers,
and photographers use
chum (a mixture of blood
and rotting fish) and baits to attract
great whites. These are among the few
sharks that stick their heads out of the
water before and, sometimes, during
attacks on prey. As the shark takes the
bait, its eyes roll back in their sockets
revealing the white surface of the
eyeball. This protects the more vital
front part of the eye from being
scratched, which may happen if the
shark was attacking live prey, such
as a seal armed with claws and teeth.

TAGGING A GREAT WHITE
Dr. John McCosker, an American shark scientist, tags a
great white off the Australian coast (top). Sonic tags have
revealed that a great white can cruise at 3 kph (1.8 mph),
travelling about 200 km (120 miles) in three days (above).

THE GOLDEN TOUCH

SATYRS
The satyrs were woodland gods; often the lower parts of their bodies resembled horses or goats. Silenus was older but, like the other satyrs, was a companion of Dionysus.

The fat satyr, Silenus, tells Midas some strange tales as he drinks his wine

GOLDEN TREASURE
This jug with coins, dating from 650-625 BC, was found in Ephesus, Turkey. The coins are made of electrum, an alloy of gold and silver used in ancient times.

THE GIFTS OF THE gods are not always what they seem. Take warning from the tale of King Midas, who thought himself wise. Midas had been tutored in the mysteries of the god of wine, Dionysus, by the poet Orpheus. So when one day some peasants brought before him an old, drunken satyr, bound with chains of flowers, Midas recognized him as Silenus, a companion of Dionysus.

Midas feasted Silenus for ten days and nights and, in return, Silenus told him many strange things. He told of a terrible whirlpool beyond which no traveller may pass. Beside it, two streams flow. By the first grows a tree whose fruit causes those who eat it to waste away. By the second grows a tree whose fruit will make men young again. One bite takes an old man back to middle age; two bites and he is a young man again; in three bites he is back in adolescence; in four he is a child; in five, a baby. Take a sixth bite, and he will disappear altogether.

At length, Midas took Silenus back to Dionysus, by the banks of the River Pactolus. The god had been missing his companion, and by way of gratitude for Silenus's safe return, he offered to grant Midas any wish he might ask for.

Midas first thought of Silenus's tale, but then he remembered a story that when he was a baby, some ants had been seen carrying golden grains of wheat and placing them between his lips – a sign of great wealth to come. So, instead of choosing youth, Midas said, "Grant that whatever I touch will turn to gold."

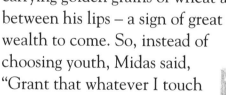

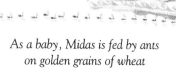

As a baby, Midas is fed by ants on golden grains of wheat

The god granted Midas's wish, and the king went away, delighted with his good fortune. He broke a twig from a low-growing branch of oak, and it turned to gold. He touched a stone and a clod of earth, and they, too, turned to gold. He gathered an ear of corn and it turned to glittering metal in his hand. He picked an apple, and it became as golden as the fabled apples of the Hesperides.

He touched the pillars of his palace doorway, and they turned to gold. Even the water in which he washed splashed golden over his hands. He called for food and wine. But when he reached for a piece of bread, it too turned to gold; when he bit into some meat, it turned to metal where his teeth touched it. Even the wine, Dionysus's discovery and gift to men, turned to liquid gold as it passed his lips.

Midas could neither eat nor drink, and soon he was in a torment of hunger and thirst. Gold, which had once been his heart's desire, was now hateful to him. He begged Dionysus to free him from his gift.

Dionysus took pity on the wretched man, and told him, "To cancel the gift, you must go to the source of the River Pactolus. Bathe in the spring there, and wash away your greed." Midas did as he was told and, as he bathed, his golden touch washed away into the river. The waters ran with gold, and even now the soil along the riverbank has a golden gleam.

WINE VESSELS
In Ancient Greece wine was a popular drink. It was believed to be the gift of the god Dionysus to mankind. Wine was often diluted, and the larger of these two bronze wine vessels would have held water for this purpose. The mixture was poured into a jug and the ladle used to fill the cups.

Midas washes away his golden touch in the river

Everything Midas touches turns to gold, including his food and wine

Robbers of the seas

W<small>HO WERE THE PIRATES</small>? Daring figures who swooped on treasure ships and returned home with golden cargoes? Brutal sea-thieves who showed no mercy to their victims? Bold adventurers who financed travel by nautical theft? In fact they were all these things and more. The term "pirate" means simply "one who plunders on the sea", but those who led this life fell into several categories: "privateers" were sea-raiders with a government licence to pillage enemy ships; "buccaneers" were 17th-century pirates who menaced the Spanish in the Caribbean; "corsairs" were privateers and pirates who roved the Mediterranean. In the words of Bartholomew Roberts, all were lured by the promise of "plenty..., pleasure..., liberty and power".

SWASHBUCKLING HERO
A few real pirates lived up to their traditional swashbuckling image. Bold and brilliant Welsh pirate Howell Davis used daring ruses to capture ships off Africa's Guinea coast in 1719.

A TEMPTING TARGET
The East Indiamen – big ships trading between Europe and Asia – provided some of the toughest but most tempting targets for pirates. In earlier times, the capture of a Spanish galleon bringing treasure from the Americas was many a pirate's sweetest dream.

Wealthy East India Companies decorated the sterns of their merchantmen — with gold

PIRATES OF THE SILVER SCREEN
Hollywood pirate films often blurred the lines between fact and fiction. In *Blackbeard the Pirate*, Blackbeard is pursued by Henry Morgan, who looks surprisingly well for a man who had in fact been dead for 30 years!

PROMISE OF RICHES
This illustration from Robert Louis Stevenson's famous pirate story *Treasure Island* shows the heroes loading sacks full of pirate treasure. Although there were many myths surrounding piracy, the vast fortunes in gold and silver captured by some pirates really existed. Pirates could become millionaires overnight, but they usually spent their booty as soon as they acquired it.

Cannon is balanced on this circular pivot

Pushing wedge in aims cannon lower

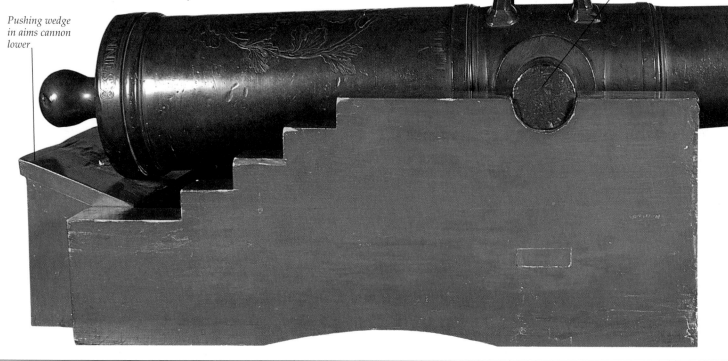

A HARD LIFE

For sailors of the 17th- and 18th-centuries, life at sea was hard and dangerous and, like "Poor Jack" in this poem, many never made it home again. Seamen were often tricked or kidnapped by press gangs into serving on men-of-war where they were subjected to appalling conditions and harsh discipline. Compared to this, a pirate's life offered freedom and easy money and many pirate crews were made up of formerly honest seamen.

"Poor Jack" going away to sea, perhaps never to return

POOR JACK.

PIRATES OF THE IMAGINATION

Pirates have captured the imaginations of many writers and artists over the years. The American illustrator Howard Pyle portrayed the pirates and buccaneers of the 17th century in colourful and authentic detail. This evocative picture epitomizes the traditional image of the flamboyant pirate captain.

A rope was attached to the end of the grappling iron

RULE OF TERROR

Pirates had a reputation for cruelty, which many of them encouraged. They knew that their victims would surrender more easily if resistance was punished by torture and death. The buccaneers in particular were notorious for their brutality.

BARBAROUS BRUTES?

The definition of a "pirate" often depended on which country you belonged to. This painting shows evil-looking Barbary corsairs attacking a helpless English crew. To the Europeans the Barbary corsairs were brutal heathen pirates, but in North Africa, they were seen as legal privateers.

DARING THE DEVIL

Popular pirate tales such as those found in Charles Elms' *The Pirates' Own Book* encouraged the "superstitious horror connected with the name of pirate". In this illustration from Elms' book a reckless pirate captain offers the devil a handful of his hair in return for a fair wind.

DANGER SIGNAL

A cannon shot was the signal for a ship to show its colours or be treated as an enemy. Pirates often tricked their victims by running up the colours of a friendly nation.

18th-century cannon that belonged to French corsair René Duguay-Trouin

GRAPPLING FOR GOLD

Swung into the rigging on the end of a rope, a grappling iron helped pirates to draw their victims' ship close enough for boarding. But pirates only did this as a last resort, preferring to make victims surrender by a show of force.

Barbed points are designed to lodge securely in the rigging of another ship

FROSTED CARROT CAKE

You will need

20 cm (8 inch) round cake tin
Baking parchment • Scissors • Sharp knife
Grater or food processor • Sieve • Large
bowl • Wooden spoon • Whisk or fork
Spoon • Skewer • Wire rack • Palette knife

For the cake

Butter for greasing cake tin

225 g (8 oz) carrots

225 g (8 oz) self-raising
flour and 2 teaspoons
baking powder

Pinch of salt

140 g (5 oz) soft, brown
muscovado sugar

Grated zest of 1 orange
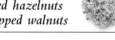

2 teaspoons ground cinnamon

115 g (4 oz) chopped
roasted hazelnuts
or chopped walnuts

55 g (2 oz) desiccated coconut

2 large eggs

150 ml (¼ pint)
sunflower oil

Juice of 1 orange

For the frosting

225 g (8 oz)
cream cheese

85 g (3 oz) butter

115 g (4 oz)
icing sugar

For the marzipan carrots

225 g (8 oz) marzipan

Orange and green food colouring

Making the cake

1 Set the oven. Grease the cake tin. Cut out a circle of baking parchment the same size as the tin and cover the base with it.

2 Scrub or peel the carrots and trim off their tops. Grate the carrots using a grater or a food processor.

3 Sift the flour and baking powder into a bowl. Mix in the carrots, salt, sugar, orange zest, cinnamon, nuts, and coconut.

4 Beat the eggs. Add the eggs, sunflower oil, and orange juice to the cake mixture and mix everything together well.

5 Spoon the mixture into the cake tin. Bake it for 60 to 75 minutes until a skewer pushed into the centre comes out clean.

6 Leave the cake to cool in the tin for 10 to 15 minutes, then remove it from the tin and put it on a wire rack to finish cooling.

Decorating the cake

1 Beat the cream cheese, butter, and icing sugar together in a bowl with a wooden spoon until the mixture is soft and creamy.

2 Spread the cream cheese frosting evenly over the top of the cooled cake, using a palette knife dipped in warm water.

3 Knead orange and green food colouring into two balls of marzipan, then mould carrots for the top of the cake.

Teatime special

Spicy carrot cake will stay fresh for several days if you store it in an airtight container.

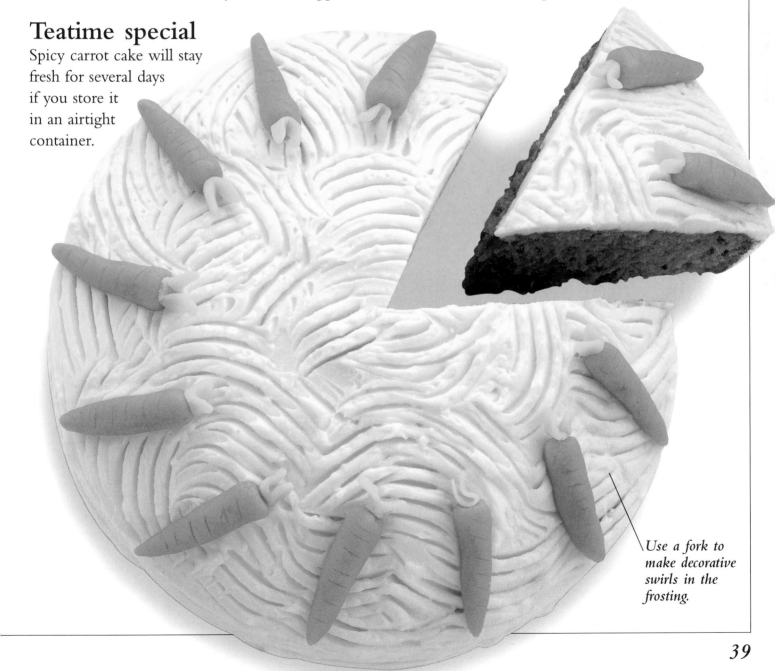

Use a fork to make decorative swirls in the frosting.

LIFEBOAT

EARLY LIFEBOATS WERE OPEN to the wind and rain. The crew lashed themselves to their seats and rowed, in constant danger of capsize, through towering waves and gale-force winds, to rescue stricken sailors. Today's lifeboats, such as this Trent class, are specially designed to skim to the rescue across the water and return home again as quickly as possible. If they capsize, they right themselves immediately. Most coastal nations have special organizations to coordinate sea rescues. One of the oldest is Britain's Royal National Lifeboat Institution (RNLI), founded in 1824.

What's in a number?

You can tell something about a lifeboat by looking at the numbers painted on its side. The first set show the boat's length in metres, or feet, depending on when it was built. The second set show whether it was the first, second, or even fifty-third of that class to be built.

Ring for safety

Life rings will keep people who fall overboard afloat until they can be rescued, but they must be hauled to safety as soon as possible. If someone is in cold water for too long, their body temperature quickly drops to a point where death becomes likely.

Seahorse-power

The engine room is the heart of any lifeboat. Trent class lifeboats are powered by two diesel engines. Each of them is more powerful than 800 horses. The fuel tanks hold 4,100 litres (901 gallons), which allows the boat to plough through the seas for more than 460 km (286 miles) before it has to be back in harbour.

Fast floaters

New lifeboats such as the Trent class are easy to maintain and have maximum speeds of up to 25 knots.

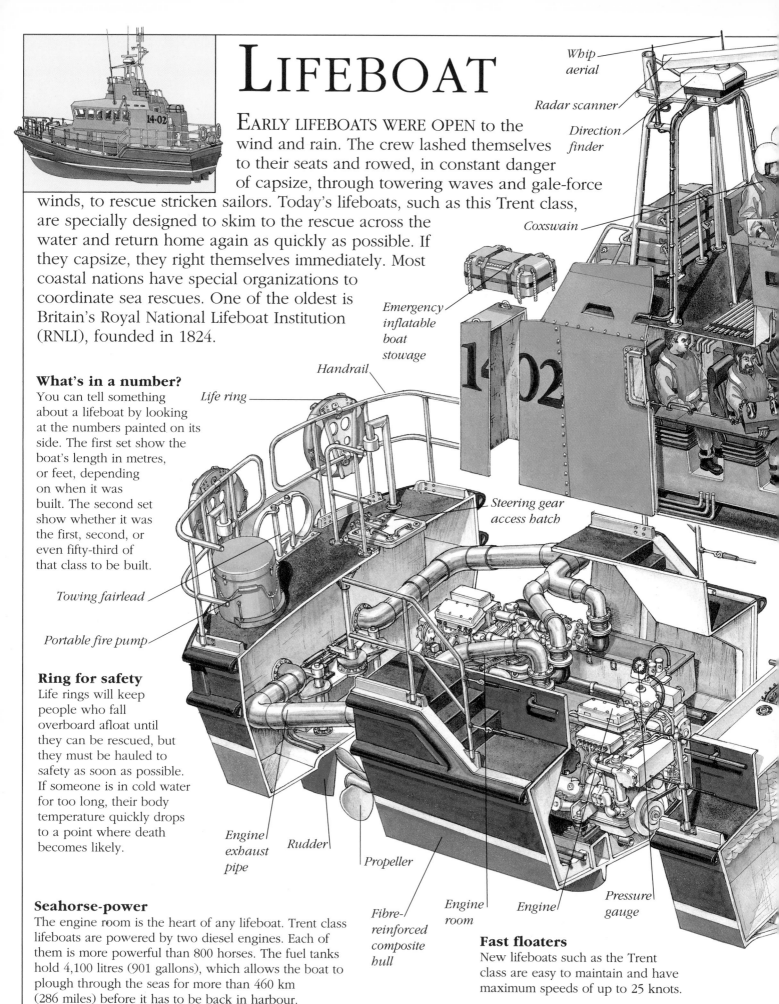

Whip aerial

Radar scanner

Direction finder

Coxswain

Emergency inflatable boat stowage

Handrail

Life ring

Steering gear access hatch

Towing fairlead

Portable fire pump

Engine exhaust pipe

Rudder

Propeller

Fibre-reinforced composite hull

Engine room

Engine

Pressure gauge

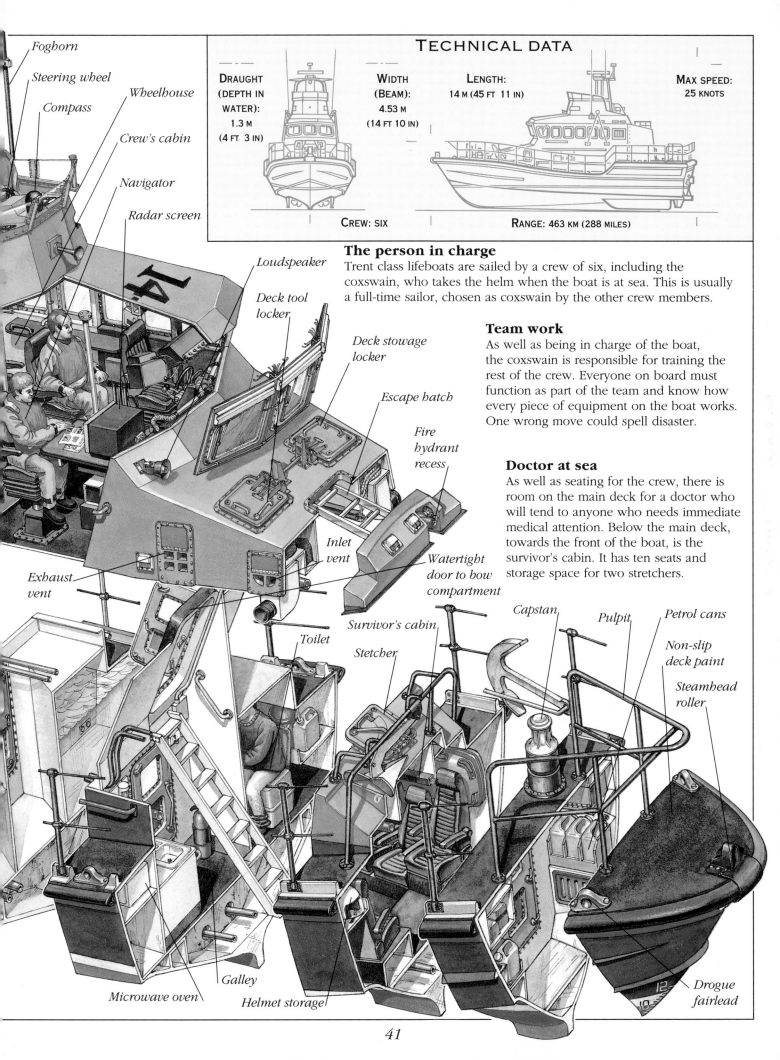

Foghorn

Steering wheel

Compass

Wheelhouse

Crew's cabin

Navigator

Radar screen

Loudspeaker

Deck tool locker

Deck stowage locker

Escape hatch

Fire hydrant recess

Inlet vent

Watertight door to bow compartment

Exhaust vent

Survivor's cabin

Toilet

Stetcher

Capstan

Pulpit

Petrol cans

Non-slip deck paint

Steamhead roller

Galley

Microwave oven

Helmet storage

Drogue fairlead

TECHNICAL DATA

DRAUGHT (DEPTH IN WATER): 1.3 M (4 FT 3 IN)	WIDTH (BEAM): 4.53 M (14 FT 10 IN)	LENGTH: 14 M (45 FT 11 IN)	MAX SPEED: 25 KNOTS
CREW: SIX		RANGE: 463 KM (288 MILES)	

The person in charge
Trent class lifeboats are sailed by a crew of six, including the coxswain, who takes the helm when the boat is at sea. This is usually a full-time sailor, chosen as coxswain by the other crew members.

Team work
As well as being in charge of the boat, the coxswain is responsible for training the rest of the crew. Everyone on board must function as part of the team and know how every piece of equipment on the boat works. One wrong move could spell disaster.

Doctor at sea
As well as seating for the crew, there is room on the main deck for a doctor who will tend to anyone who needs immediate medical attention. Below the main deck, towards the front of the boat, is the survivor's cabin. It has ten seats and storage space for two stretchers.

Mammals

Hanging fruit bat

Q1. Are bats completely blind?

Q2. What do you call the offspring of a male donkey and a female horse?

Q3. Why does a squirrel monkey have such a long tail?

Q4. What does a hedgehog do when it's alarmed?

Hedgehog

Q5. What is the female elephant in charge of a herd known as?

Q6. Can a sea otter sleep in the water?

Q7. What is the difference between an African elephant and an Indian elephant?

Q8. How does a porcupine defend itself when it's in danger?

Q9. From what are elephant tusks made?

Q10. What is a koala's favourite food?

Q11. What makes a mammal a mammal?

Q12. What ape can make its own tools?

Q13. Why do horses have to wear metal shoes?

Q14. How long does a dormouse hibernate: 2 months, 4 months, or over 6 months?

Q15. How do zebras protect themselves from lions and other predators?

Q16. Why do elephants flap their ears so much?

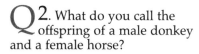

Dugong

Q17. What is another name for dugongs and manatees?

Q18. How long is an elephant's pregnancy: 12 months, 18 months, or 22 months?

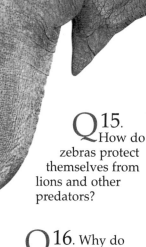

An Asian elephant

Q19. What is a marsupial?

Q20. Do mammals lay eggs?

Q21. In which continent would you find the small chinchilla rodent?

Q22. Which mammal lives, breeds, sleeps, and eats underground?

Palomino with Western-style bridle and saddle

Rat cleaning itself

Q23. How often can a female rat reproduce: every 4 weeks, every 6 weeks, or every 8 weeks?

Q34. Bats are the only mammals that can fly. True or false?

Q24. What does a herbivore eat?

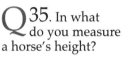

Sperm whale

Q35. In what do you measure a horse's height?

Q25. What colour was Moby Dick, the sperm whale in Herman Melville's novel?

Q36. What is a baby hare called?

Q26. Which are more closely related to humans: apes or monkeys?

Q37. What does a skunk do when it's attacked?

Q27. Why are giant pandas in danger of becoming extinct?

Q38. Which large, furry mammal spends all day hanging upside down in trees in the rainforests of South America?

Q28. Is a monkey a primate?

Q39. Which country has the most elephants: Zaire or Congo?

Q29. Who lives in a warren: a rat or a rabbit?

Q40. How do rams defend their territory?

Q30. Which is the smallest mammal?

Q41. Which is the largest deer: a moose or a caribou?

Q31. Why do some mammals like to groom each other?

Q42. Can bears swim?

Q32. How does a hamster store food?

Q43. What does a beaver build?

Q33. What are the 4 ways a horse moves?

Black bear

Q44. What colour does a weasel's fur turn in snowy, cold climates?

JUGGLING

HERE IS A WAY TO AMAZE YOUR FAMILY and friends. Juggling three balls with two hands is easy when you know the method. Once you have mastered basic juggling, you can try the following show ideas or learn some other skills that go well in a juggling show.

Juggling Hints

Practise a little every day, and don't stop until you have achieved something new.
If you drop a ball while performing, just smile and blame it on "a sudden gust of gravity"!
You can add yo-yo tricks or skipping to your show for variety.

How to make juggling balls

1 Gather 80 g (3 oz) dry rice into a mound on a double square of plastic foodwrap. Pull up the corners to make a neat parcel.

2 Use a pair of scissors to cut off the neck of a round balloon. You will need three balloons for each juggling ball.

3 Stretch open one of the balloons and pull it over your rice parcel. Then pull the second and third balloon over the parcel.

Repeat Steps 1 to 3 to make three equal weight and size balls.

LEARN TO JUGGLE

It will take you 20 minutes to learn to juggle if you spend five minutes on each of these simple exercises.

Focus on the balls when they reach the top.

As this ball peaks, throw the other ball.

Try to throw the balls to roughly the same height.

Throw with your weaker hand first. Later, swap over.

  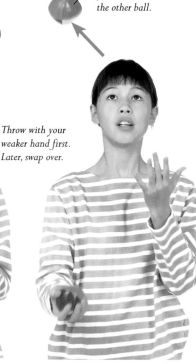 

Exercise one
Hold a ball in each hand and throw them both up at once, slightly higher than your head. Practise until you ALWAYS do good throws and good catches.

Exercise two
Imagine two bells in the air above your hands. Throw the balls up to make a "ding, dong, catch, catch" rhythm. Later, do "dong, ding, catch, catch".

Exercise three
Toss the balls, one by one, diagonally across your chest. The rhythm is "criss, cross, catch, catch". Now you're ready for real juggling – the three-ball cascade.

Exercise four
"Criss-cross" starting with your left hand. As the second ball peaks, make a third toss from your left hand, then the fourth from your right, and so on ….

Juggling with one hand is easy. Just throw one ball straight up and throw the second when the first one peaks.

You must carry each scarf up and across your body. It is hard work!

★ DIABOLO
This ancient Chinese toy spins at speed on a string. Use one hand to pull on the string and make the diabolo spin. Experts can throw and catch it, and do lots of other tricks.

If the diabolo tilts, the control (pulling) string can push or pull it level again.

★ JUGGLE LUNCH
Use two balls and an apple. Occasionally juggle two balls in one hand while taking a bite of the apple. It looks funny if you bite the wrong one.

★ JUGGLE SCARVES
Juggling scarves lets you juggle in slow motion. Use large, light, nylon scarves or soft plastic bags that drift through the air.

You won't be able to hold two big balls in one hand, so get a friend to throw in the first flying ball.

★ FLOWER STICK
Use the two hand sticks to gently toss a Flower Stick from side to side in mid-air. It looks magical.

Catch and "lift" the Flower Stick just above its centre point. Don't hit it hard.

Throw your ball high in front of your partner's furthest shoulder.

Scoop the ball upwards with a big open hand.

★ HUGGLING
Huggling is easy. You and a friend each become one arm of a very wide person, then juggle normally.

★ JUGGLE BIG BALLS
Start your show juggling three tiny balls and work your way up in size until you are juggling basketballs.

DIGITAL DRAGONS

Computer special effects have changed the look of cinema forever. Instead of creating models of dinosaurs and space creatures in the studio, cutting-edge technology can create these three-dimensional images on a computer, making them look as realistic as the actors with whom they share the screen. From the eye-popping T-rex attack in *Jurassic Park* (1993) to the gently floating feather in *Forrest Gump* (1994), computer-generated images – CGi – now dominate every aspect of modern filmmaking. New techniques such as motion capture, pixel-stretching, morphing and wire-framing are extending the frontiers of CGi by the day, taking the cinema-goer into a whole new world of big screen magic.

Wings must be constructed with different wire frames to show them stretched out wide in flight or tucked into body

Special attention was given to Draco's face, which was given the same facial expressions as Sean Connery, who supplied the voiceover

"Viewpaint" software technology allows the operator to paint spines and scales on the dragon's body

DRACO THE DRAGON
In the film *Dragonheart* (1997) a dragon-slaying knight teams up with the last of the dragons to battle an evil ruler. To make the fire-breathing creature look realistic, special effects technicians scanned a 1.5 m (4 ft) model into a computer and then constructed a virtual dragon on screen. Digital computer wizardry was used to make Draco the dragon breathe fire, as well as talk and interact with the actors in the film.

COMPUTERIZED MONSTERS
Creating a dragon on the computer involves intensive research and painstaking attention to detail. First, a three-dimensional image, called a "wire frame", is created on screen. This is done by using specific digital lines connected to key parts of the dragon's body to form a digital skeleton. Then a special software program is used to mould the dragon's muscles, which will make it appear to move realistically, around the frame. Finally, "Viewpaint" technology is used to paint the dragon on screen, giving it the computer-generated skin, bone, and flesh of a living, breathing creature.

Wire frame is built up in stages and animators give life to the data by moving the measurements frame by frame

Dragon's tail can be enlarged or decreased in size by stretching the lines and body points of the wire frame

Digital measurements must be exact and in scale with the whole image

To make the dragon stand upright on its haunches, the computer experts measure the feet and legs against the body to give the correct height reading

Background footage is filmed months in advance, and is then combined with the computer generated dragon in the final film

The dragon's eyes are modelled on those of a lizard, and are digitally created using special software to make them blink, move, and close shut

The dragon's mouth and snout will be digitally animated to show facial expressions and breathe CGi fire

Skin textures, shadows, and body armour are all painted on the wire-frame dragon as if painting a 3-D model

Shooting skills

A BASKETBALL GAME is won by the team with the most points, and you can only get points by shooting the ball through the basket. Every team member can score, so developing your shooting skills is vital. There are different types of shots, and you will need to learn several different techniques if you are to become a regular scorer for your team. The type of shot you take will depend on your situation. If you are standing still with the ball and are within shooting range, you can take a set shot or a jump shot. If you are able to dribble up to the basket, you can take a lay-up shot.

The set shot

You will be stationary when you make a set shot, so your stance is very important. Stand with your knees slightly bent and the ball held in front of your chest, just under your chin. Hold your shooting hand behind and slightly under the ball, with your fingers spread and pointing upwards.

Hold the ball with both hands.

If you are a right-handed shooter, place your right foot slighly farther forwards than your left foot.

The lay-up shot

You should perform a lay-up shot when you are on the move, after catching a pass or when dribbling towards the basket. This sequence of pictures shows a player moving to take a lay-up shot. He has approached the basket from the right, having dribbled the ball with his right hand.

Holding the ball
When you hold the ball for a shot, do not touch the ball with the palms of your hands, use only your fingers.

3 Your left foot is your take off foot for your jump upwards and towards the basket. You should start lifting the ball up in front of you as you start your shooting action.

1 When you are within range of the basket for a lay-up shot, gather the ball in both hands while both your feet are off the ground. Bring your right foot down to land.

Move at a good pace.

Keep your eyes on your target.

Your left foot takes the second and final step.

Bring your right leg forwards as you prepare to jump from your left foot.

2 Look up to the basket as your left foot comes forwards to land. Remember that you are only allowed to take two steps when you are holding the ball.

Your arms should reach up towards the basket.

As you start the shot, straighten your legs.

Release the ball with a strong flick of your wrists and fingers.

Make the action one continuous movement.

For longer shots, you may lift your feet off the floor.

Releasing the ball
You must reach up so that you release the ball as close to the basket as possible.

The flight of the ball should continue to a target point on the backboard.

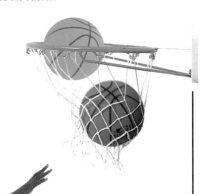

If you hit the correct spot on the backboard, the ball will rebound into the basket.

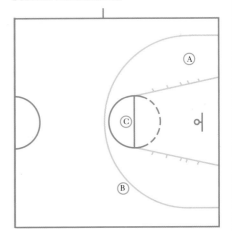

Take your left hand away from the ball just before you shoot with your right hand.

Your shooting arm should be fully stretched.

Point the fingers of your shooting hand upwards.

Stretch up your arms.

Concentrate on the target until your shot goes in.

Jump off the opposite foot to your shooting hand.

Jump as high as you can.

6 Gently guide the ball up towards the target so that it drops softly into the basket. If you are a beginner, move towards the basket at an angle of 45° to the backboard. You will see a gap between the ring and the backboard through which it is easier to aim the ball at the backboard. Try varying your angle of approach as you become more skilled.

Scoring points
The number of points you get for a goal depends on where you took the shot from. A field goal (a goal scored from open play as opposed to a penalty shot) taken from point A, within the three-point line, is worth two points. A field goal scored by a player at point B, with both feet behind the three-point line, is worth three points. A free throw (a penalty shot awarded for a rule infringement) taken from point C is worth 1 point.

4 To get more lift when you jump, drive your right knee upwards. Hold the ball with your shooting hand behind and slightly under it. Your other hand should be at the side of the ball, giving it support.

5 Just before releasing the ball, you should be at full stretch and be holding the ball as high as possible. Aim the ball at the small rectangle on the backboard, at a point just inside the top corner closest to you. If you hit that target, the ball should rebound into the basket.

HAUNTED BUILDINGS

Most haunted houses have a tragic history. Borley Rectory, often called "the most haunted house in England", is haunted by the ghost of a nun who was murdered in the 17th century. Houses with a happy atmosphere are rarely haunted. However, a few do have a resident ghost – usually someone who was so attached to the house that they wanted to stay.

BORLEY RECTORY

Borley Rectory, in Essex, UK, had several ghosts, including its first vicar, the Rev Henry Bull, who built the Rectory in 1863. Other spirits included a phantom nun and a ghostly coach that could be heard rattling up the drive. Many residents complained of poltergeists, including one vicar who was hit on the head with a hairbrush. After Borley Rectory mysteriously burned down in 1939, a woman's skull was found buried in its cellar. Could it have belonged to the phantom nun?

Borley Rectory,
Essex, UK

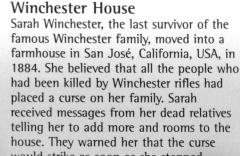

Sarah Winchester's house, San José, USA

Winchester House

Sarah Winchester, the last survivor of the famous Winchester family, moved into a farmhouse in San José, California, USA, in 1884. She believed that all the people who had been killed by Winchester rifles had placed a curse on her family. Sarah received messages from her dead relatives telling her to add more and rooms to the house. They warned her that the curse would strike as soon as she stopped building. Sarah's ghost now haunts the corridors of the rambling mansion that she took 38 years to build.

Haunted Churches

There are probably as many haunted churches as haunted houses. The ghosts are usually those of a priest or a monk kneeling at the altar. This well-known photograph (above) seems to show the ghost of a priest. It was taken in St Nicholas's Church in Arundel, Sussex, UK. Cameras often seem able to capture figures that are invisible to the eye, or which appear only as a faint blur of light.

House of Faces

In a house in Bélmez de la Moraleda, Spain, mysterious faces appear on the concrete kitchen floor. The first face appeared on 23rd August 1971. It was removed and the floor was laid with fresh cement. However, other faces immediately took its place – at one point there were no fewer than nine faces. The house had been built over a graveyard and ghost experts concluded that the faces were made by poltergeists. More recently the "House of Faces" has become a place of pilgrimage to those who believe that the faces are supernatural portraits of saints.

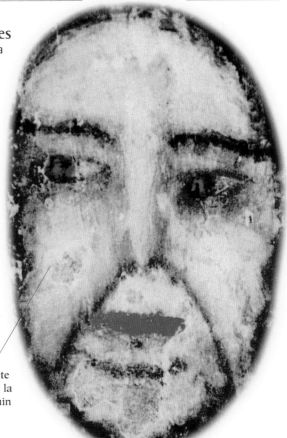

The expression seemed to change

Face on a concrete floor, Bélmez de la Moraleda, Spain

> ## "I was glad to get away."
>
> A visitor to Borley Rectory

The Raffles Hotel, Singapore

Raffles Hotel

The Raffles Hotel, one of the oldest hotels in Singapore, was haunted by the sound of a girl's voice singing an English nursery rhyme. The voice has been heard by hundreds of people. The hotel was built in 1897 on the site of a girls' boarding school, so the voice may be that of a long-dead pupil. The ghostly singer has not been heard since the old hotel was renovated in the 1980s. Her identity remains a mystery.

Amityville Hoax

The house in Amityville, Long Island, USA

A house in Amityville, Long Island was once the most famous haunted house in the USA. In 1974, Ronald DeFeo killed six members of his family there. In 1975, the Lutz family moved in but left after only a month. They claimed that they had been driven out by phantom footsteps, horrible smells, and ghostly hands. A book based on George Lutz's story, *The Amityville Horror*, became a best seller. However, the story proved to be a hoax. The family had left, unable to pay for the upkeep.

ATLANTIS

GOD OF THE SEA
This bronze head of
Poseidon is part of a
statue dating from 450
BC. Zeus's brother, the
god of the sea, the lake,
and of the earthquake,
Poseidon was one of the
most powerful of the
immortals. He was often
shown wielding a trident,
a three-pronged weapon
used by tuna fishermen.

SHADES OF ATLANTIS
Ancient ruins lying
beneath the waters of
a mountain pool in
Pamukkale, Turkey,
bear witness to quick-
tempered Poseidon's
destructive power.

THE GREEKS HAD many legends of the distant past: of Phoroneus, the first man, and of Deucalion and Pyrrha, who survived a flood sent by Zeus to rid the world of evil men. But when the Greek statesman Solon related these tales to the priests of ancient Egypt, they laughed. "You Greeks know nothing of your own history. You talk of one flood, but there have been many. It was in such a flood that your ancestors perished!" And the priests told Solon the story of the island of Atlantis, from where, nine thousand years before, the noblest race of men that ever lived ruled most of the known world.

A poor couple named Evenor and Leucippe once lived on a rocky island with their daughter, Clito. Poseidon, god of the sea, was smitten by Clito's beauty and married her. He then reshaped the island to make it a dwelling fit for his new bride.

He fashioned it into a series of circular belts of sea and land, with an island at the centre that basked in sun and beauty. The rich plains brought forth wheat, fruit, and vegetables in abundance, the forested hills sustained all kinds of animals – even herds of elephants – and beneath the soil were many precious ores.

Clito bore Poseidon five sets of twin boys. They were all kings, and the oldest, Atlas, was the high king, and his sons after him. The beautiful kingdom came to be called Atlantis.

*The beautiful kingdom of Atlantis is a series
of belts of land connected by bridges*

The people of Atlantis were wise in the arts of peace and war and soon ruled all the peoples of the Mediterranean. All of the island's kings added to the country's store of riches. The outer wall of the city of Atlantis was coated with brass, and its inner one with tin. The palace at the centre, with Poseidon's temple, was covered in gold. The buildings were built of white, black, and red stones: sometimes all one colour, sometimes in intricate patterns. A great harbour was opened up to the sea, and bridges were built between the belts of land.

Thus was Atlantis, in the days of its greatness.

For many years, the ten kings ruled wisely and well, each passing on his wisdom to his heir. But as generation succeeded generation, the kings' divine blood grew thinner and they fell more and more under the sway of mortal passions and worldly desires. Where once they had valued precious things simply for their beauty, they now fell prey to greed. Where once the people had lived

Poseidon stirs up a tidal wave to engulf the city of Atlantis

together in friendship and harmony, they now squabbled over power and glory. Great Zeus, seeing this favoured race descend day by day into the pit of human ambitions and vices, rebuked Poseidon for allowing such a thing to happen. And Poseidon, in sorrow and anger, stirred up the sea. A huge tidal wave engulfed Atlantis and the island sank for ever beneath the waters.

Where it lies, no one knows for certain – nor whether, under the ocean, Poseidon's children once more walk the streets of Atlantis in peace and wisdom, or if only the fishes play among the sea-worn bones of this fabled city.

The great city of Atlantis lies beneath the waves

❖

THE REAL ATLANTIS? Archaeologists believe Atlantis may have been the island of Stronghyle (Santorini) in the eastern Mediterranean. Around 1500 BC, a volcanic eruption submerged the island.

OAK TREE

THIS TALL, MAJESTIC OAK TREE MAY HAVE lived for up to 600 years, its spreading branches reaching up to 30 m (100 ft) high. Oak wood is prized for its strength and has been used for centuries to build palaces and galleons, treasure chests and thrones. Yet an oak starts life as a tiny acorn, no bigger than a thumbnail, and it has to survive many dangers. Insects, birds, and squirrels eat acorns, and even if one takes root, it may be eaten or trodden on. These mighty giants of the forest have a tough childhood!

Foliage feeders

Oak leaves provide food for insects. A big oak can support up to 400,000 caterpillars at once. It defends itself from too much insect attack by quickly replacing eaten buds and producing a bitter chemical, called tannin, which repels insects.

Foodmaking leaves

Leaves make nutrients (the tree's food) using a green chemical called chlorophyll. In sunlight, each leaf photosynthesizes. This means that the chlorophyll makes nutrients from minerals and water brought up from the tree roots, and from air taken in through tiny holes, called stomata, in the leaves. The food and water are sent to and from the leaf through its veins and its stem.

Oak galls

Many oak trees have wart-like growths on them called galls. They are caused when insects lay their eggs somewhere on the oak and secrete substances that make tree cells grow around the eggs. This helps both the insect and the tree. The gall surrounds the larva (growing insect) so that it can't attack the rest of the tree, while the larva gets food and shelter inside the gall. Birds peck at galls to get at the larva inside.

Marble gall

Oak-apple gall

OAK GALL

Gall wasp

Common spangle gall

Gall wasps

There are many types of gall. The oak-apple gall is one of the most common. It is caused by a wasp that lays its eggs in leaf buds in spring. The oak-apple grows round the egg.

Jay

Stock dove

Redstart

Wryneck

Chaffinch

Blackcap

Rook

Red kite

Turtle dove

Golden oriole

Song thrush

Magpie

Blue tit

Pied flycatcher

54

All about bark
The bark is the rough outer layer of the tree. It helps prevent damage from animals, stops the oak from drying out, and protects it from heat and cold. As the tree grows thicker, its bark stretches and splits.

Tauny owl

Oak bark beetle

Gallery made by oak bark beetle

Great spotted woodpecker

Garlic snail

Sulphur tuft fungi

Stag beetle larva

Blusher

Slug

Stag beetle

Song thrush

Lynx

Nuthatch

Starling

Purple emperor

Wood warbler

Polecat

Common shrew

Acorn

Mole

Yellowneck mouse

Grey squirrel

Spindleshank fungus

Dryad's saddle

Root gall

Wood pigeons and nest

From the acorn
Acorns are the fruit of the oak tree. Each acorn grows in a cup attached to a twig. The hard acorn shell protects the soft seed inside. Only one in a million acorns survives to become a tree. The rest are eaten by animals such as insects, squirrels, and jays. In the Middle Ages farmers took their pigs into the forest to graze on the fallen acorns.

BIRTH OF A TREE

Birth of a tree
Stage 1: In spring the seed inside a fallen acorn sends a root down into the soil. The root sucks up water and minerals. **Stage 2:** The seed sends up a shoot into the light and two rounded seed leaves open out to reveal a tiny bud. **Stage 3:** As the first proper tree leaves grow, the roots lengthen to find more nutrients. In autumn the leaves fall, leaving a new bud that will start to grow in the spring.

Feeding a tree
In spring and summer the roots suck up water and minerals to help produce the tree's food. In autumn and winter any unused food is carried back down to the roots to be stored underground until the spring. The roots also support the tree; oak roots are particularly strong so the oak can withstand centuries of storms and high winds.

Fab fungi
Fungi are plants but they do not contain chlorophyll and so cannot make food by photosynthesis. They take their food from decaying or living things, including oaks. Spindleshank fungus, shown above, anchors itself to an oak's trunk. Fungi are spread by tiny seeds called spores.

STAGE MAKE-UP

WITH GOOD STAGE MAKE-UP you can create really convincing characters. Try to copy some of these faces, using the basic techniques and special effects outlined below. Once you've got the face, you can put on a show.

BASIC TECHNIQUES

It is best to use water-based make-up or face paints. You can use cheaper make-up for details, but if you are sponging a layer of colour over your whole face, you should get a good quality "pancake", which comes in a flat, round container.

1 Start with a clean face. Test the face paint first on a small area to make sure you are not allergic to it.

2 Apply a base paint with a damp sponge, using long careful strokes. Blend in a second colour.

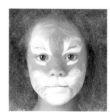

3 Use different colours and a fine brush to paint in details such as whiskers and lips.

Gel and powder the hair to blend in with the rest of the statue.

Remember to paint the neck and shoulders, too, if they are going to show.

Use a draped white sheet for a stone statue costume. You could paint "cracks" on it to make it look more realistic.

★ HUMAN STATUE

Put on a waxworks show with living statues. Pose the "statues" around a room on pedestals. They should keep very still, although if you want to give someone a fright, one of them could suddenly "come to life".

★ TIGER

Enter on all fours, with the slinky movement of a cat. Your trainer gives orders, but you do the opposite. In frustration, she asks you to hold a hoop, while she shows you what to do. You stand up and applaud when she jumps through the hoop.

★ PIRATE

Pirates are fierce and adventurous. You could do a pirate show packed with exploring, kidnapping, and swashbuckling action.

★ CHINESE OPERA SINGER

Traditional Chinese operas have complicated plots about princesses, bandits, emperors, and animals. Create your own opera, and include dancing to Chinese music and kung fu movie-style stunts.

★ FROG

"The Frog Prince" is a famous story by the Brothers Grimm. You could turn it into a play or make up an ecology show about a frog that wants to preserve its pond.

SPECIAL EFFECTS

You can use special make-up wax to create bumps, wrinkles, and warts. Cereal flakes make good scabs, and raspberry jam is convincing blood.

Looking old

It is easy to add 70 years to your face with make-up. But don't forget to change the way you walk and talk, too.

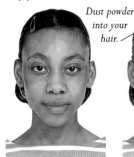

Dust powder into your hair.

1 Look in the mirror to see where the natural lines appear on your face.

2 Draw dark lines along these lines. Highlight either side with lighter paint.

Warts and scabs

If you are a warty witch or the victim of a mysterious plague, you will need some help from the make-up department.

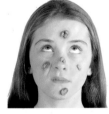

1 Stick cereal flakes or puffs on to your face with small pieces of wax.

2 Paint the flakes to suit the face. Add a touch of red for an oozing sore.

Gash

Need to look like an accident victim? Special-effects wax and fake blood come to the rescue!

1 Smooth a lump of wax on to your face with water.

2 Make a well in the middle and fill with fake blood.

★ CLOWN

Make up your own clown routines. You will find creating funny routines easier if you have a "straight" partner such as a Ringleader, schoolteacher, or parent.

A clown face can be really colourful and decorative. This one has glitter gel on it to give it sparkle.

Paint a big, colourful smile, much bigger than your real mouth.

Countries of the world

The Eiffel Tower rises 300 m (984 ft) above Paris.

1 Most neighbours
Which of these countries is the nation that has the most neighbouring countries?
■ Saudi Arabia
■ Russia
■ China

Australia was once part of the British Empire.

A red London bus.

2 Smallest country
The smallest country in the world is the Vatican City. Which famous person lives there?

3 Largest country
The ten largest countries are:
■ Russia   ■ Australia
■ Canada   ■ India
■ China   ■ Argentina
■ United States   ■ Kazakhstan
■ Brazil   ■ Sudan
Four of these countries' flags are shown on these two pages. Which are they?

4 Most tourists
Countries with the most tourists each year are:
■ France   ■ United Kingdom
■ Spain   ■ Hungary
■ United States   ■ Mexico
■ Italy   ■ Poland
■ China   ■ Austria
Which country would tourists visit to see the Eiffel Tower?

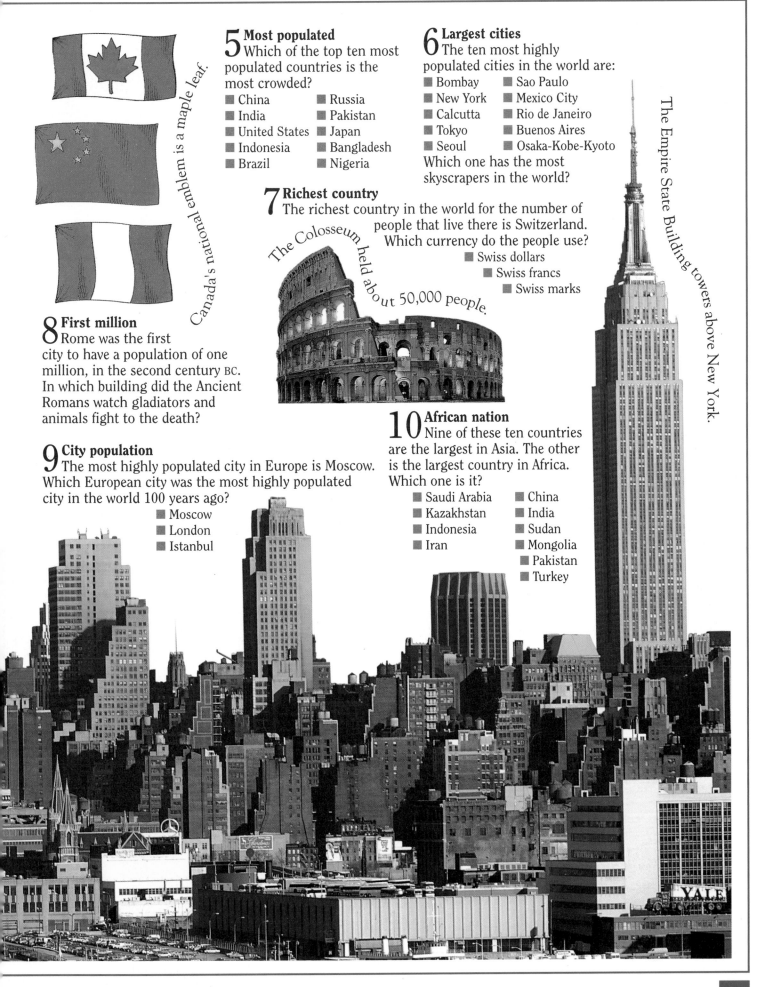

Canada's national emblem is a maple leaf.

5 Most populated
Which of the top ten most populated countries is the most crowded?
- China
- India
- United States
- Indonesia
- Brazil
- Russia
- Pakistan
- Japan
- Bangladesh
- Nigeria

6 Largest cities
The ten most highly populated cities in the world are:
- Bombay
- New York
- Calcutta
- Tokyo
- Seoul
- Sao Paulo
- Mexico City
- Rio de Janeiro
- Buenos Aires
- Osaka-Kobe-Kyoto

Which one has the most skyscrapers in the world?

7 Richest country
The richest country in the world for the number of people that live there is Switzerland. Which currency do the people use?
- Swiss dollars
- Swiss francs
- Swiss marks

The Colosseum held about 50,000 people.

8 First million
Rome was the first city to have a population of one million, in the second century BC. In which building did the Ancient Romans watch gladiators and animals fight to the death?

9 City population
The most highly populated city in Europe is Moscow. Which European city was the most highly populated city in the world 100 years ago?
- Moscow
- London
- Istanbul

10 African nation
Nine of these ten countries are the largest in Asia. The other is the largest country in Africa. Which one is it?
- Saudi Arabia
- Kazakhstan
- Indonesia
- Iran
- China
- India
- Sudan
- Mongolia
- Pakistan
- Turkey

The Empire State Building towers above New York.

Environment friendly

TECHNOLOGICAL PROGRESS HAS provided us with many advantages, and will continue to do so in the future. But there is a price to pay – the damaged ozone layer and the effects of greenhouse gases may have terrible consequences for the future of our planet. Air pollution is causing acid rain, and water contamination is killing wildlife. Some natural resources are rapidly being used up, and many large tracts of rainforest have been destroyed. Because of our actions, some of the animals we shared the planet with are extinct, while others are endangered. If we do not take a more responsible attitude towards our finite resources, the results will be catastrophic.

VISIONS OF THE FUTURE
Creating your own artificially controlled environment once seemed an exciting prospect. Some architects have taken great pleasure in designing future homes, such as this one from the 1950s, which rotates to face any direction. Protected by a climate-conditioned dome, it would be possible to enjoy summer activities in the middle of winter. Such schemes can be seen today in holiday parks and leisure centres.

Lightweight body means engine has to do less work and so requires less fuel

IDEAL FOR THE CITY OF THE FUTURE
The motor car is a very popular form of transportation. But people are concerned at the levels of pollution and the future scarcity of petrol. Manufacturers are therefore designing cars for city use with clean, fuel-efficient engines.

ALTERNATIVE TO FUEL
Scientists around the world are searching for alternatives to non-renewable and expensive fossil fuels. Alcohol, which is made from distilled grain, is one alternative to petrol. It has been a success in countries without natural oil reserves.

Honda's solar car in the World Solar Challenge Race

POWERED BY THE SUN
A solar-powered vehicle uses solar cells to convert energy from the sun into electricity, which drives its electric motors. Yet solar cars are still little more than expensive novelties. However, solar cells are likely to play a major role in the future generation of electricity.

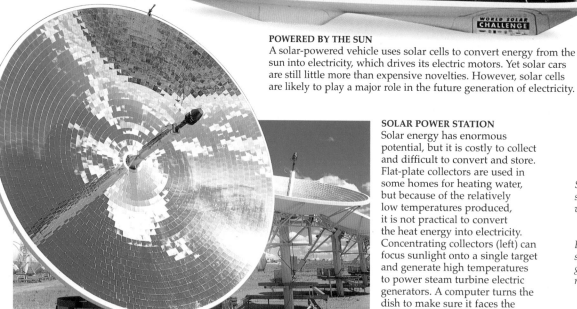

SOLAR POWER STATION
Solar energy has enormous potential, but it is costly to collect and difficult to convert and store. Flat-plate collectors are used in some homes for heating water, but because of the relatively low temperatures produced, it is not practical to convert the heat energy into electricity. Concentrating collectors (left) can focus sunlight onto a single target and generate high temperatures to power steam turbine electric generators. A computer turns the dish to make sure it faces the sun throughout the day.

Streamlined shape prevents wind traps

Building supported by giant tripod megastructure

RECYCLING

Increasingly, people are becoming aware of the value of recycling. Today, we generate an enormous amount of waste, and there are increasing problems with its disposal. In the future, we will manufacture products that are built to last, and can be repaired. They will be easily dismantled for sometimes surprising reuse (right), or at least disposed of safely and efficiently.

Worn rubber tyres are not safe to use

Tyre ready to be re-formed after shredding

Handbag made from shredded car tyre

Hot, stale air ventilates through louvre at the top of the building

In winter, warm air at the top is used to heat cold air coming in at the bottom

Air between glass skins is heated by solar radiation

OFFICES IN THE 21st CENTURY

Most traditional offices are not environmentally friendly. They consume high levels of energy in winter, and require even more to keep them cool in summer. They often lack a natural source of air and light, and so need electric lighting switched on all day. This not only results in high fuel costs, but is also unpleasant for the occupants. As the cost of fuels rises, energy-inefficient office buildings will need to be redesigned. This remarkable-looking office building has been designed to address exactly these problems – maximizing the use of both natural ventilation and light.

Mirrors reflect natural light deep into offices

Air-conditioning is replaced by a natural ventilation system

Building stands high above ground, away from pollution

Quiz answers

16-17 Inventions: 1850-1950

1 They were the first to fly an aeroplane.

2 The fax machine; an early form of fax machine called the pantelegraph was installed in France in 1856. The telephone was not invented until 1876.

3 It played for 23 minutes.

4 It was introduced in 1920.

5 Pneumatic (inflatable) tyres. They had been invented in 1845 and "reinvented" in 1888, but the Michelins were first to make them for cars, in 1895.

6 The meter; it was not new to the world, for the Romans fitted a kind of meter to carts long ago.

7 The Model T Ford; the assembly line had earlier been used to make clocks and watches.

8 Germany; Karl Benz made a motorized tricycle in 1885 and had built a 4-wheel car by 1893.

9 Germany; it opened in Berlin.

10 About 1930, in the United States.

11 The gramophone, an early record player.

12 In 1885, by Gottlieb Daimler in Germany.

13 The helicopter; the first practical helicopter was built in 1936, the first jet aeroplane in 1939.

14 He invented it in 1938.

15 The airship, in 1852. The first glider flew in 1853, but controlled flight in a glider didn't happen until 1891. The aeroplane first flew in 1903.

16 In London, England.

17 30 tonnes (29.5 tons).

18 In 1920, in the United States.

19 It had a red and green light. Amber came 4 years later.

20 He was American.

21 The cash register.

22 In 1926, invented by John Logie Baird.

23 False; the first practical lightbulb was invented in 1879, the electric iron in 1882.

24 In 1872; chewing gum was an old Native American idea.

25 In 1946; but microwaves in the home did not appear until 1955.

26 Guglielmo Marconi; in 1894 he was sending radio waves across the room; by 1901 he was sending messages across the Atlantic.

27 It was invented in 1857.

28 It only played 1 tune.

29 Coca-Cola, launched as "the esteemed brain tonic and intellectual beverage".

30 Tuned into a radio broadcast.

31 On a squash court, in the United States, in 1942.

32 It recorded and reproduced sound.

33 In 1950, for use in restaurants.

34 The ballpoint pen.

35 In 1914, called the "hookless fastener".

36 The electric refrigerator.

26-27 The human body

1 100,000 times each day.

2 Children; they have around 300 more bones than adults. In adults, bones fuse together.

3 Tooth enamel is the hardest substance.

4 3 litres (5 pints) of air.

5 China; in 1989 there were reported to be 61,929.

6 Keratin is found in nails, hair, and skin.

7 A baby develops in the uterus, or womb.

8 The skin is the largest organ.

9 Sigmund Freud; he treated patients by listening to them talk about their dreams and thoughts.

10 The ribcage protects the chest organs.

11 It can only bend forwards and backwards.

12 The small intestine, measuring 6.5 m (21 ft). The large intestine is 1.8 m (6 ft) long (it is thicker).

13 Over 600 muscles.

14 This is true.

15 In 1895.

16 In the spine.

17 The head weighs around 4 kg (8.8 lb).

18 In the 19th century.

19 They are made up of protein foods.

20 A gastroscope is used to examine the stomach.

21 The femur; it is found in the thigh.

22 Louis Pasteur; he led the way for the development of antiseptic surgery.

23 206; half of them are in the hands and feet.

24 Marie Curie.

25 A local anesthetic numbs a part of the body but a general anesthetic makes a patient unconscious.

26 Alexander Fleming, in 1928.

27 To carry blood from the heart around the body.

28 Doctors believed that too much blood in the body was a cause of disease.

29 In 1876; she was a campaigner for the admission of women to the professions.

30 It was forbidden by the Church to dissect bodies for scientific study.

31 Amputate shattered limbs.

32 The major blood groups are A, B, AB, or O.

33 Over 200 muscles.

34 This form of medicine is called acupuncture.

35 Louise Brown was born in England in 1978.

36 In the ear; it is the stirrup.

37 It was performed in 1967.

38 In the 19th century.

39 Bile aids digestion.

40 A midwife delivers babies.

41 A stethoscope is used for this.

42 In 1853; devised by Charles Plavaz in France.

43 There are 27 bones in the hand.

44 It was set up in 1948 to act as an information centre concerning health problems facing the world.

45 They are attached to the sternum or breastbone.

46 They are sight, smell, taste, hearing, or touch.

47 When we are cold, tiny muscles lift the body hairs to trap warm air.

48 In the 1840s. Patients were made unconscious by nitrous oxide, ether, or chloroform.

42-43 Mammals

1 No; bats have perfectly good eyesight.

2 The result is a mule.

3 To help balance itself when walking the branches high up in the treetops.

4 A hedgehog rolls into a ball to protect its belly.

5 The matriarch, responsible for the herd's safety.

6 Yes – it lies on its back and wraps itself in seaweed so it won't be swept away by the current.

7 African elephants are bigger, with larger ears.

8 A porcupine turns its back on its foe, rattles its quills, grunts, and then reverses into its enemy.

9 A hard substance called ivory.

10 The koala will only eat the leaves of certain eucalyptus trees.

11 A warm-blooded animal with fur that gives birth to live babies and feeds its young on milk.

12 Chimpanzees can do this.

13 To protect their hoofs from damage.

14 Over 6 months in cold climates.

15 They graze in groups; their stripes make it hard for lions to pick out an individual from the herd.

16 To keep themselves cool in hot weather.

17 Sea cows, which graze on sea plants.

18 22 months, longer than any other animal.

19 An animal with a pouch in which to carry babies.

20 Only the platypus and the echidna lay eggs.

21 In the mountains of South America.

22 The mole.

23 Every 4 weeks.

24 Herbivores only eat plants.

25 Moby Dick was white.

26 Apes are more closely related.

27 Giant pandas eat mainly bamboo; large areas of bamboo forest in China have been cut down.

28 Yes; along with apes and humans. Primates have large brains.

29 A rabbit lives in a warren.

30 Kitti's hog-nosed bat; it weights 0.5 oz (1.5 g).

31 For social reasons, as well as for fur care.

32 Hamsters "carry" food in cheek pouches.

33 Walking, trotting, cantering, and galloping.

34 True; their wings are really webbed hands.

35 In hands; a hand equals 10 cm (4 in).

36 A baby hare is called a leveret.

37 It sprays a horrible smelling liquid at enemies.

38 A sloth; it moves very slowly and only wakes up at night.

39 Zaire (but estimates of elephant numbers vary).

40 Run at each other and clash heads and horns.

41 A male moose may weigh 450 kg (1,000 lb).

42 All bears can swim and are happy in water.

43 Beavers build dams to stop flowing water.

44 A weasel grows a white coat in snowy winters.

58-59 Countries of the world

1 **Most neighbours**
China. It has 16 neighbours: Afghanistan, Bhutan, Hong Kong, India, Kazakhstan, Kyrgyzstan, Laos, Macao, Mongolia, Myanmar, Nepal, North Korea, Pakistan, Russia, Tajikistan, and Vietnam.

2 **Smallest country**
The Pope. The Vatican City has an area of 44 ha (108.7 acres). It has its own governor, post office, coinage, and law courts.

3 **Largest country**
Argentina, Australia, Canada, China. Every country has its own flag.

4 **Most tourists**
France. The Eiffel Tower was built in Paris, France, in 1887-1889. It was designed for the centennial Paris Exhibition of 1889.

5 **Most populated**
Bangladesh. It has 841 people per sq km of land.

6 **Largest cities**
New York. The word "skyscraper" was first used to describe a building in the 1880s, when the first tall office block of 10 storeys or more was built in Chicago, United States.

7 **Richest country**
Swiss francs. Swiss banks are used by rich people from all over the world to escape taxation.

8 **First million**
The Colosseum. When it first opened, in AD 80, the Colosseum's arena could be filled with water, and "sea battles" were fought by gladiators in small ships.

9 **City population**
London. A hundred years ago, London had a population of 4,231,431. The most highly populated city in the world today is Tokyo, with a population of 28,447,000.

10 **African nation**
Sudan. It borders the Red Sea and has an area of 2,505,581 sq km (9,674,048 sq miles).

Acknowledgements

All the spreads in the DK Annual 2000 originally appeared in the books listed below:

Junior Chronicle of the 20th Century
A new millennium (pp 4-5)
Text: Simon Adams, Robin Cross, Ann Kramer, Haydn Middleton, and Sally Tagholm

Disaster!
Hindenburg (pp 6-7)
Text: Richard Platt
Illustrations: Richard Bonson

Painting: A Young Artist's Guide
Technique and texture (pp 8-9)
Text: Elizabeth Waters and Annie Harris
Photography: Dave King

The Young Soccer Player
Goalkeeping (pp 10-11)
Text: Gary Lineker
Photography: John Garrett

The Children's Step-by-Step Cookbook
Snacks on sticks (pp 12-13)
Text: Angela Wilkes
Photography: Dave King

Special Effects in Film and Television
Larger than life (pp 14-15) and Digital Dragons (pp 46-47)
Text: Jake Hamilton
Photography: Geoff Brightling and Andy Crawford

1001 Questions & Answers
Inventions: 1850-1950 (pp 16-17), The human body (pp 26-27), and Mammals (pp 42-43)
Text: Helena Spiteri and David Pickering

Eyewitness Guides: Space Exploration
How to be an astronaut (pp 18-19)
Text: Carole Stott
Photography: Steve Gorton

Polar Exploration
The great escape (pp 20-23)
Text: Martyn Bramwell
Illustrations: Marje Crosby-Fairall and Ann Winterbotham

Eyewitness Guides: Insect
Beetles (pp 24-25)
Text: Laurence Mound
Photography: Colin Keates, Neil Fletcher, Frank Greenaway, Harold Taylor, Jane Burton, Kim Taylor, and Oxford Scientific Films

Big Bang
Birth of the Milky Way (pp 28-29)
Text: Heather Couper and Nigel Henbest
Illustrations: Luciano Corbella

Factastic Book of 1001 Lists
The Olympic Games (pp 30-31)
Text: Russell Ash

Eyewitness Guides: Shark
The great white shark (pp 32-33)
Text: Miranda Macquitty
Photography: Frank Greenaway and Dave King

The Illustrated Book of Myths
The Golden Touch (pp 34-35) and Atlantis (pp 52-53)
Text: Neil Philip
Illustrations: Nilesh Mistry

Eyewitness Guides: Pirate
Robbers of the seas (pp 36-37)
Text: Richard Platt
Photography: Tina Chambers

Children's Quick & Easy Cookbook
Frosted carrot cake (pp 38-39)
Text: Angela Wilkes
Photography: Amanda Haywood, Clive Streeter, Norman Hollands, and Dave King

Look Inside Cross-Sections: Rescue Vehicles
Lifeboat (pp 40-41)
Text: Louisa Somerville
Illustrations: Hans Jenssen

Showtime!
Juggling (pp 44-45) and Stage Make-up (pp 56-57)
Text: Reg Bolton
Photography: Andy Crawford

The Young Basketball Player
Shooting skills (pp 48-49)
Text: Ian Smyth with a foreword by Eduardo Perez
Photography: Andy Crawford

The Unexplained: Ghosts and the Supernatural
Haunted buildings (pp 50-51)
Text: Colin Wilson
Photography: Andy Crawford, Gary Ombler, and Sarah Ashun

Richard Orr's Nature Cross-Sections
Oak tree (pp 54-55)
Text: Moira Butterfield
Illustrations: Richard Orr

Top 10 Quiz Book
Countries of the world (pp 58-59)
Text: Russell Ash

Eyewitness Guides: Future
Environment friendly (pp 60-61)
Text: Michael Tambini
Photography: Andy Crawford and David Exton

Picture credits
The publisher would like to thank the following for their kind permission to reproduce their photographs:

Key: a=above, b=below, c=centre, l=left, r=right, t=top

Allsport: 30-31 c; **Ancient Art & Architecture Collection**: 37 cr; **Bridgeman Art Library, London/New York**: 52 tl; **Camera Press John Reader/ILN**: 28 bc; **Bruce Coleman Ltd**: 25 bc, 25 cbr; **Mary Evans Picture Library**: 37 tr, 50-51 b, 51 tl; **Fortean Picture Library**: 51 c, 51 tr; **Ronald Grant Archive**: 36 cl, 51 cr; **Robert Harding Syndication/IPC Magazines Ltd**: 24 tl; **Hulton Getty**: 7 cra; **Image Bank**: 4 bl; **Kobal Collection**: 14 cl; **Moviestore Collection**: 14 tl; **NASA**: Front jacket cl, 18 cl, 18 c, 18 br, STSCi 29 cl, 29 tl; **National Museums & Art Galleries on Merseyside**: 36 tl, 36 cr, 37 tl; **POLYGRAM**: 14 tr, 14-15, 14 c; **Popperfoto**: 4 br, 6 tl; **Rex Features**: 5 b, 60 cr; **Science & Society Picture Library**: 61 tc, 61 tr; **Science Photo Library**: 4 tl, 5 tr, David Hall 60 cl, John Mead 60 bl; **Frank Spooner Pictures**: 5 c; **Scott Polar Research Institute**: 20 tl, 22 tl, 23 br; **Topham Picturepoint**: 50 tr; **Vintage Magazine Company Ltd**: 60 tl

The publisher would also like to thank:
Andreas Von Einsiedel, Andy Crawford, British Museum, Colin Keates, Dave King, Florence Nightingale Museum, Geoff Dann, Gillian Ayres, Glasgow Museum, Hans Jenssen, Jane Burton, John Garrett, John Heseltine, Kieron Parris, Luciano Corbella, Martin Anastasi, Mike Dunning, Musee de St Malo, Museum of Natural History of the University of Florence Zoology Section, "La Specola", National Maritime Museum, National Motor Museum, Beaulieu, Natural History Museum, Nilesh Mistry, Ray Moller, Richard Bonson, Richard Orr, Royal Academy of Arts, London, Sharon Peters, Smithsonian Institute, Steve Gorton, Susanna Price